Instant Opinion

Over 100 of the best political posts from

sjhoward.co.uk

S. J. Howard

Instant Opinion

Over 100 of the best political posts from sjhoward.co.uk

ISBN: 978-1-84753-446-0

For the last four years, I've been writing political commentary, yet I'm utterly unqualified to do so. I'm a medical student by day, and I have no greater political insight than anyone else with a good grasp of current affairs. Despite this, my writing has proven to be very popular. I am a political blogger.

It's very easy to dismiss political blogging as uniformed, ephemeral, and driven by gossip – and it is often all of those things, but that makes it a no less valid contribution to the political debate than anybody else's. The great strength of blogging is its immediacy, and reflection of the mood of the real people in politics – the people on the street, rather than the people in power.

In effect, it provides instant opinion.

Blogging will never replace reports by well-informed political journalists, and nor will it replace opinion pieces by erudite social commentators. It is more a new media 'letters page', where individuals can make their views known in an uncensored and unedited form, whilst inviting comment and debate from other individuals. It gives a platform to individual voices, but not the whole platform.

My reasons for blogging are nothing to do with furthering the cause of citizen journalism, trying to prove a political point, or trying to impart great wisdom. I blog because I enjoy writing, and this medium allows me to develop my own writing style and publish things to a worldwide audience whenever I want. Quite often, that audience will respond, and hence I'll develop as a writer. It's something I enjoy, and it helps me to relax.

This collection of some of my political writing has been brought together to celebrate four years of continuous blogging. I hope that reading it brings you as much pleasure as writing it brought me. And remember that there is always fresh writing on my website at sjhoward.co.uk.

Happy blogging!

Simon Howard, April 2007

Comment is free, but facts are sacred

CP Scott, 1846-1942

Contents

The Labour Party

The Labour Party, the current party of Government, won an historic third term in 2005. The election campaign, however, brought out what I felt to be some of the worst aspects and traits of New Labour, as will be seen over the coming posts.

Party Websites

Compare for a moment the website homepages of the country's two biggest political parties, just weeks before an anticipated General Election.

The Conservative homepage tells me that they think immigration limits are the way forward, that homeowners, rather than burglars, should be protected by the law, and that they have clearly set out policies for action on tax, schools, hospitals, crime, asylum, and immigration. It carries only two small mentions of the Labour Party.

The Labour Party homepage tells me that the Tories are bad. It tells me nothing *at all* about Labour policies. In fact, the Tory party takes up the second-biggest headline on the page. And the only pictured party leader is Michael Howard. There's isn't a Labour member in sight.

And yet, despite hiding their policies away beneath a thick layer of Tory-bashing, Labour is *ahead* in the opinion polls, and roundly predicted to win the next general election.

Who said that intelligent discussion is the way forward for politics?

/ Posted 6th February 2005

Labour reveals election pledges

These are bizarre election pledges. Not least because of the lack of verbs that makes them read like something a five-year-old would've written. Let's take each one in turn…

Your family better off

This is clearly not English, but I'm assuming it means something along the lines of my family having more money under a Labour government. I'm not entirely sure how this can come true. I'm a medical student. If I'd qualified as a doctor in 1997, when Labour came to power, I'd have had debts of £7,697. As things stand, it looks like I'll have debts of £19,248 when I qualify and want to set up home. Mr Blair's plans to introduce university top-up fees will make this nearer £64,000 for new medical students. So how, exactly, does he plan to make my family - that of a young doctor - better off?

Your family treated better and faster

How can you treat a patient 'better'? I don't know how Mr Blair plans to measure that, but it'll probably involve more arbitrary targets. The introduction of targets on waiting times now means that most GP practices will no longer accept appointments in advance. You have to beat the mad rush on the phone in a morning to get an appointment for the same day. Not only does this mean that many urgent cases get pushed to the back of the queue whilst everyday problems get quick appointments, it also discriminates against those without a phone line, which are likely to be those of a lower socioeconomic class whose health should be a top priority for the government. Why is Mr Blair promising to treat patients faster, instead of in a more appropriate order?

Your child achieving more

I certainly wouldn't want children of mine to be £64,000 in debt when they start their first job, so I'd probably steer them away from a medical career. Is that helping them to 'achieve more'? And this government has decreed that teachers should have ten percent non-contact time - that's ten percent of the time teachers are supposed to be teaching should be spent doing paperwork away from the children. How does that help children to achieve more?

Your country's borders protected

From what? If, like the Conservatives, he's talking about asylum seekers, then surely (given that he's in power for eight years) he should be defending the situation he's created, not saying 'Well, it's a bit rubbish, but we'll try and fix it up next time. Honest, guv'.' And why do we need 'protecting' from asylum seekers anyway?

Your community safer

This government has completely failed to get a handle on rising violent crime levels. Why should I believe that Mr Blair can get a grip on the problem when he's failed to do so for eight years? Or has violent crime only just become a priority? Has he been preoccupied bombing Iraq - effectively committing violent crime of his own - until now?

Your children with the best start

This is one area on which I actually admire Labour's record. They've done excellently in setting up schemes like SureStart and the Child Trust Fund that make a real difference in poorer areas of the country.

I'd also like to know why Labour are *still* going out of their way to continually attack the Tories. On the day the pledges are announced, a large portion of their website's homepage is still dedicated to ridiculing the Conservative leader - on this occasion, over a perfectly well considered view on ID cards. Do Labour not believe in anything themselves? Are they only striving to be better than the Tories, and nothing more?

/ Posted 11th February 2005

Hain: Vote Lib Dem, get Tories

Today, the Guardian has published a comment piece by Peter Hain, the leader of the Commons and the secretary of state for Wales. It essentially tells us not to vote for the nasty parties, who have all these terrible plans, and yet, amazingly, fails to mention *even once* what Labour would do differently.

There isn't a single mention of Labour's future policies in this article. There's a fair bit of selective picking-and-choosing of the best bits of what Labour has achieved in the past, but not a hint of the future. And only one fleeting mention of their party leader - which is more than he gets on the Labour party homepage, where the only party leader pictured is Michael Howard.

The best bit is where Mr Hain decides that he'd like to tell me what I believe:

> The truth is, even our most ardent Guardian critics agree with 95% of what Labour has done, in particular building the strongest economy in living memory and record public investment.

If Labour wins on a campaign of 'Everyone else is mean, vote for us' then it's going to make the British public as foolish as were the Americans for voting for George Bush. Unless Labour step-up their game, they're just going to look increasingly silly, and lose an election that six-months ago they had in the bag.

/ Posted 28th March 2005

The Chancellor's budget speech

Because the General Election has yet to be formally declared, matters of State continue, including the announcement of the Chancellor's Budget earlier today.

> Mr Deputy Speaker: Stability the foundation. Investment not cuts. Every child the best start in life.

I think I missed something early on in Mr Brown's speech: What's the new tax rate on verbs? It must be pretty high if even the Chancellor can't afford them.

There's little in the speech itself to disagree with - there rarely is in a pre-election budget, I suppose. I just wonder how he can manage to announce tax cuts, borrowing cuts, and yet massive spending increases. I'm no expert on the economy, but to me that says 'tax rises after the election'.

The main feeling that I took away from today's events was how much better Mr Brown would be as Labour's leader: Tony Blair's fake emotion and anger versus Mr Brown's real commandeering and forceful delivery, appearing to actually believe what he says. I know who I'd choose.

Overall, not a fantastic day for Labour, but not a bad one either. A couple of days of positive reports in the newspapers might give them a bit of a boost, but I think lots of the tabloid press will instead concentrate on picking holes and making Labour look bad.

So all-in-all it's probably been a pretty neutral day. Not exactly what Labour needed right now, but not so bad that it makes Mr Brown look bad… probably a reasonably good day for him personally.

/ Posted 16th March 2005

Lies, Damn Lies, and Labour

Today, Labour have launched a new election poster which boldly announces

INTEREST RATES HALVED WITH LABOUR

From this poster, you might get the impression that interest rates have halved under Labour. An easy mistake to make, I agree. Sadly, though, it isn't true. When Labour came to power, the interest rate was 6.25%. It's now 4.75%. If Mr Brown thinks that 4.75 is half of 6.25, then how on earth are we supposed to trust his budgets?

The Conservatives have produced some proposed budget figures that you can argue about, but they have a pretty clear explanation of how they've done their calculations and why they've done them that way. And, as it happens, they haven't used the figures that would show Labour in the worst light: They've tried to be as logical as possible using the next-to-useless government figures produced by Labour. Their crime ads are blatantly misleading, though, and quite a disappointment because of this. But, by my count, Labour are still streets ahead on the number of blatant lies they've told during this pre-election campaign. But then, Alan Milburn said he'd do anything to win. Labour should be ashamed.

/ Posted 2nd April 2005

Show me the new money!

You can't possibly have missed the fact that Ruth Kelly, the Education Secretary, has promised £280m worth of 'new money' for school meals. This was very kind of her, and obviously nothing to do with the fact that with Jamie Oliver was on Mr Blair's doorstep.

But the truth will out, and usually quite quickly in an election campaign, so no-one was really surprised when Mr Blair later admitted

> Of course it is part of the education budget, but it is still new in the sense that this is money now specifically allocated to school meals.

So does this make it new money? No. They're playing that age-old game of announcing the same money again and again. They've announced the education budget, and now they announce a subsidiary of that, claiming that it's new money. As far as I can see, 'new' money is money that has not previously been announced.

But, of course, if I announce 'I will spend a whopping £2 on fruit each day', and then another day announce 'I have £1 of new money to increase the apple budget', most people would take away the message that I'm going to spend £3, which is good for public perception when my fruit-buying opponent announces that he is to spend only £2 on fruit. But, of course, we would both be spending only £2, it's just that I've announced my apples budget separately from my fruits budget, and so made the whole thing look like it's worth more than it really is.

But then, isn't that New Labour policy through-and-through?

/ Posted 31st March 2005

Labour's Manifesto

I've had little more than a flick through the Labour manifesto, but one thing immediately jumped out at me:

> **New Labour's record: The contract delivered**
>
> **Our country is changing for the better, because we fulfilled the promises of our 1997 and 2001 manifestos.**

This jumped out for two reasons: Firstly, it's in absurdly large type. Secondly, it's not true: It's another Labour lie. Let me demonstrate using some quotes from the manifestos whose promises they apparently fulfilled:

We will now give British people the final say in a referendum on the single currency. Did I miss it?

We will now reform the appointments system so that by the end of 2005 every hospital appointment is booked for the convenience of the patient making it easier for patients and their GP to choose the hospital and consultant that best suits their needs. This will not be delivered anywhere near on time.

We want to help the Post Office keep up with the best in a fast-changing market. And closing hundreds of branches was part of this plan?

We will not introduce 'top-up' fees and have legislated to prevent them. Top-up fees are on the way – and what happened to this 'legislation' when they managed to introduce them?

By 2004, patients will be able to see a GP within 48 hours. Can you?

Same day tests and diagnosis will become the norm. The fastest I've ever seen an out-patient blood test come back is 48hrs – and that's one of the commonest and simplest tests.

We will give every citizen a personal smartcard containing key medical data giving access to their medical records. Have you got yours?

The Criminal Records Bureau will help stop paedophiles and others who are a danger to children from working with them. Except it didn't work for the Soham girls, did it?

By 2004 we are pledged to reduce teenage pregnancy by 15 per cent. Complete and utter failure.

So, given that the first jump-out page of the new manifesto is a lie, which other bits are also lies?

/ Posted 13th April 2005

Campbell thinks it's all over

Tony Blair, following his spring conference epiphany, claimed that he and the party were no longer arrogant. Now it's not that I'm doubting that, but I'm not entirely sure how else to characterise Alistair Campbell's announcement that 'the job is largely done' a little under two weeks before polling day, and a little over half way though the campaign.

When will Mr Blair realise that Mr Campbell is more of a liability than an asset? And when will Mr Campbell realise that Mr Blair is more of a liability than an asset? They should all, as usual, be ashamed. And should certainly not receive your vote.

/ Posted 26th April 2005

Somehow, despite the general feeling in the country about Mr Blair, Labour won an historic third term in office. Despite this, the negativity I felt towards them didn't improve.

Dirty government incentivised

In my opinion, one of the worst aspects of the Blair government is that ministers who resign in disgrace are almost invariably rehired, making a mockery of the idea of resigning because it's the 'right thing to do', and removing all honour associated with standing down because you're not worthy of office. What had never occurred to me until today, thanks to a good journalist asking an intelligent question of the Prime Minister's Official Spokesperson, is that these ministers get payoffs for resigning from their posts, and then get rehired. And, on top of that, there's no wish to reform the system.

So not only is there no honour to resigning in disgrace any more, but it's actually incentivised. The politician who's done something so inescapably bad that they are forced into resigning gets a nice fat pay-off, and then is rehired. So they are, effectively, paid for being naughty. Even Dr Tanya Byron can see that's not a good idea. And, frankly, it's disgraceful.

Look at Estelle Morris, for example. Her mistakes put thousands of teenagers' life plans off course, and caused untold worry and stress in families across the country. So she resigns, apparently very sorry for the mess she's made. And I truly believe she was sorry - she seems a very open and honest woman. And yet, I guess it's not all that difficult to be truly sorry when you know you're going to get a nice big pay-off and a job back in government, with the associated huge salary, within a matter of months.

Tony Blair may have aspired to heading the washing-powder 'whiter-than-white' government, but his government is, at the very least, as soiled as the last. He should be ashamed.

/ Posted 25th June 2005

A tale of 500,000 illegal immigrants

During the election campaign, Mr Blair said

> You cannot determine specifically how many people are here illegally

He even said it was impossible to estimate the number. I know, because I sat and watched the interview when he made these claims.

Also during the election campaign, John Salt came up with a figure of 500,000 illegal immigrants, which ministers called

> Grossly inaccurate

Of course, how they knew it was inaccurate when they were unable to make the calculations themselves is a mystery.

Now it's quite understandable that the Labour party would be a little coy about admitting that 500,000 people are in the country illegally when an election is being fought in which immigration and asylum are central themes.

Yesterday, though, the Home Office declared that there are approximately 570,000 illegal immigrants in the country. Which is, no doubt, a help when we're debating an ID cards bill, which is (nonsensically) supposed to tackle illegal immigration.

Clearly confused, some bright spark asked the Prime Minister's Offical Spokesperson if it had come as a surprise to the Prime Minister that Home Office were able to produce statistics on illegal immigration given that he had said that such figures were impossible to calculate. The reply? That Tony Blair could not possibly have known the figure during the interview because it hadn't yet been calculated. So why he said it was *impossible* to calculate, nobody really knows.

Putting to him that this was convenient that this figure had not been available during the General Election but was now being used to justify ID Cards didn't get anybody much further. The PMOS simply replied that the figures were not being used to justify ID cards, and…

> In all of this we should not lose sight that asylum applications are down 73% from the peak of October 2002.

See what he did there? He jumped from immigration to asylum, despite condemning the Tory party during the election for confusing the two in people's minds. In answer to a question quite clearly about immigration, he tells us that asylum applications are down!

But we really shouldn't be surprised at all this. Tony Blair's public image no longer matters as he's not seeking re-election, and thus is not accountable to the wider electorate any more. He can do what he likes, and get the dirty work done without having to worry about looking bad in public. And what did Alan Milburn say during the campaign?

> I'd do anything to win the election.

Guess what? He has.

/ Posted 1st July 2005

Blair's apology

I know a Blair apology is a rare old thing, but I'm not sure that the poor people who are being asked to pay back tax credits they received due to government errors, despite the fact that they can't afford to do this, are terribly grateful.

And, in a classic Blair non-apology, he didn't apologise for the error itself, but for the 'hardship or distress' it caused. Which could easily have been avoided if his government had simply drawn a line under its own mistake, instead of effectively penalising those on the receiving end of the error.

And then he launched into a speech about why tax credits are normally wondrously marvellous things, and that the whole system is basically perfect except for this one small error, that's resulting in people having to live on £56 per week. He's not even suggesting any way of helping these poor people out.

He should be ashamed of himself, and he should take some action to sort this mess out, not try and brush over it with a vacuous apology and self-congratulation. Pathetic.

/ Posted 22nd June 2005

Labour lies about pensions reform

On the *Today* programme this morning, some Labour official or other insisted that the pension reforms they'd come up with were designed to be 'non-partisan' and they hoped to reach a 'cross-party consensus', not play party-political games. The claim was repeated on *The World at One*, and quite possibly on many other news broadcasts throughout the course of the day. Of course, making such claims simply sets up clear criticism of any party who dares to point out flaws in the white paper on pensions, so really it's a good strategy. If only they stuck to it.

Unfortunately, they didn't. Tonight, I received an email from the Labour Party:

> The proposals we are publishing today represent the greatest renewal of our pensions system since the post-war reforms implemented by Clement Attlee's government... Since 1997, we have made real progress in tackling the appalling legacy of pensioner poverty we inherited from the Tories, so far helping a million pensioners out of poverty.

Non-partisan? I think not. Why is it that even when they think they're doing the right thing, the Labour spin machine just can't help pumping out lies? And how can they say they've had 'real progress on pensioner poverty' when Council Tax has soared, and OAPs imprisoned for failing to pay? I just don't get it.

Mr Hutton's changes mean that I will be working until I'm 68. That's fine, I have nothing against working into old age. I mean, most 68-year-olds can't set a video recorder, and I'll no doubt have a similar incompetence when it comes to the medical breakthroughs and technologies of the 2050s, but I'm sure that won't be a problem. And when I'm taking your blood or excising some growth,

I'm sure you won't be too worried about my small tremor. And at the end of a twelve-hour shift, I'm sure you'll forgive my aging brain for prescribing a drug that just happens to react with something else someone else gave you.

Of course, working to 68 will allow me to earn the money to cover the student debts that Labour have given me - otherwise my net income over my working career would be reduced.

Not that much of it matters anyway: Predictions are that there will be 3,000 junior doctors unable to find suitable training posts by the time I qualify. If I never get a job, I'll never have to retire. Now there's a cheery thought.

/ Posted 25th May 2006

How and why is Clarke still in office?

Charles Clarke's department allowed 1,023 criminals who should have been considered for deportation to roam free around the country, with some of them committing further offences.

He knew about this for *three weeks* before he bothered to let the Prime Minister know about it, let alone the Police who need to track these people down.

Even after three weeks, he *still* didn't even know the scale of the problem, or whether any of the prisoners had reconvicted.

And yet, he's stayed in office thus far on the basis that he's the best person to fix a problem *he created*. And the longer he stays, the more reports continue to trickle out, and the more damage it does to a Labour government already facing a grim local elections result.

What *is* he doing? And why hasn't he been unceremoniously booted out?

He clearly can't stay as Home Secretary. That's now absolutely obvious and as clear as clear can be. But in any reshuffle, there's really no cabinet position of equal power to that of Home Secretary. Foreign Secretary or Chancellor would be a promotion, which would make Mr Blair look arrogant beyond belief. Anything less than those two positions would be a demotion, which Clarke would never agree to. So what's going on?

If Clarke resigns tomorrow, it'll hit the papers on Wednesday, the day before the local elections. That's not satisfactory. He could resign at the point of a reshuffle, but he's a clever guy - why hang on that long and keep the bad press coming? If he was going to go, from a political point of view he should have done it by now.

So what's missing? There's an outside chance that Tony Blair could use the local election result to announce a date for his departure, and relieve Gordon Brown of his Chancellorship to concentrate on the handover of power. Charles Clarke could sneak in and be caretaker Chancellor, which would technically be a promotion, but no-one would care because the story would be eclipsed. Patricia Hewitt could be shuffled out of Health at the same time.

Prescott's a stickier problem, because Deputy Leader isn't a job Mr Blair gets to play with - it's elected by the Labour Party at large, but again the announcement of Blair's departure would overshadow any news about Prescott's pants anyway.

It all seems a bit unlikely, but there's *something* that doesn't add up here.

/ Posted 1st May 2006

Who dares slap Prescott?

The Right Honourable John Leslie Prescott is to have his 'wrists slapped' for staying at Philip Anschutz's ranch and failing to declare an interest when handling the same Philip Anschutz's business over the Millennium Dome (until bullied into it, of course). My question: Given Mr Prescott's history of 'hands-on' politics, who is going to stand there and give him a good slapping?

Those unfamiliar with Westminster disciplinary proceedings may be somewhat lost. The system works thusly:

- The perpetrator of horrendous, intolerable offences, like taking a two-week part time job whilst not in cabinet without consulting the correct committee is punished with immediate sacking.
- Major offenders, who have committed such crimes as disagreeing with the Prime Minister, are treated to a humiliating 'You've let me down, you've let the Party down, and most of all, you've let yourself down' speech until eventually forced out of the clique and out of the cabinet.
- If you're a little bit naughty and abuse your power by sleeping with your secretary, you go over the PM's knee and have a couple of departments taken off you, but keep your job, salary, and perks.
- If you do something minor, like accepting gifts and holidays from someone before then giving them governmental support (let's just call corruption), then you get a quick slap on the wrist.
- If you do something barely worth mentioning, like, y'know, lying to Parliament or starting an illegal war, then that's just brushed under the carpet and ignored.

See, it all makes perfect sense. *All we need now is someone good at ducking!*

/ Posted 19th July 2006

From Teflon Tony to Slippery Johnny

I know I've asked this before, but just how is John Prescott still in office? He's lost his job yet kept his salary and perks, slept with his secretary, punched a voter, done allegedly dodgy political deals without declaring an interest, been photographed playing croquet when he should have been working, been roundly mocked for having two jags, and yet *still* appears to be quite happily in office. People said Tony was made of Teflon because nothing every stuck: Well this is one Slippery Johnny, with no-one ever quite able to pin him down long enough for him to lose his job.

Even if, as it is rumoured, he has some good dirt on Tony Blair and so can't be fired, he must be able to see the damage he's doing the government and the Labour party, and want to resign in the best interests of a turbulent, troubled party which needs less scandal, not more. Surely he can't be seriously thinking about disrupting the smooth and orderly transition by running for PM himself, because there's far too much dirt on him already.

He can't keep on going like this forever: Johnny must split from the government soon, if only so the party gives an appearance that it's doing something. Or is this a greater problem with New Labourites, as we saw with Charles Clarke? They're so obsessed with themselves that they won't resign for the greater good: They have to be pulled off the government scene in a most undignified way?

/ Posted 6th July 2006

The next leader of the Labour Party, and hence the next Prime Minister, looks likely to be Gordon Brown. Despite the Labour Party's best efforts, however, I tend to think that the 'transition of power' will be less 'stable and orderly' than they would like.

MPs' fury at Blair and Brown

It appears I've been misjudging the story of the division between Tony Blair and Gordon Brown. According to The Guardian today, a rivalry far more bitter than that which I had imagined does indeed exist between these two, and they really are employing the most puerile tactics to attack each other (such as giving different speeches simultaneously and blaming each other), and helping to destroy the party in the process.

I thought they were more intelligent than that.

This certainly cannot be good for the country. United leadership is effective leadership. Of course, how you define effective is open to opinion (I am certainly no fan of the New Labour agenda), but one reaches one's goals most effectively when one's team is united against a common enemy. The lack of a strong enemy is probably what has brought about the infighting in the first place: With no-one in particular to attack, Brown and Blair attack each other.

With the Conservative Party's history, it is a little difficult for them to launch a sustained moral attack on a warring leadership, which leaves the door open for Charlie Kennedy and the Liberal Democrats. If he can make big enough gains in the forthcoming election, then he could easily hold the balance of power.

Of course, the other possibility in all of this (though I accept that the chances are practically zero) is that Mr Brown launches an all-out assault on the Prime Minister now, delaying a General Election until much later in the year, or even into next year, with him leading the party. Or, possibly, somebody else leading them.

Whatever's going on here, it's damaging to Labour. And if Michael Howard doesn't give a convincing and strong performance at this week's PMQs, then he's not worth his salt. Mr Blair should be looking pretty silly come Wednesday afternoon.

But there's a silver lining here for Mr Brown: He has clearly shown himself to be in touch with the majority of the electorate… We're told he doesn't believe a word Mr Blair says.

/ Posted 11th January 2005

Brown pleads over petrol prices

In an entirely bizarre move, Mr Brown has been pleading with oil producing companies to up their production, so that petrol prices don't hit £1/litre. Why he needs to do this pleading when two-thirds of the petrol price is down to him, I don't really understand.

For every penny more the suppliers charge, the price goes up a total of 3p, thanks to 2p in tax. So if Mr Brown is so desperate for the petrol prices not to rise, then why can he not reduce the proportion of tax charged, so that the total revenue remains consistent instead of increasing? That way, the impact of any increase would be reduced by two-thirds. Heck, he could even *reduce* the total revenue if he's so worried about petrol prices.

I guess we can only be glad that, as reported by the BBC today:

> his comments did little to placate fuel protesters, who said demonstrations planned for Wednesday would go ahead unless Government ministers agreed to meet them to discuss their concerns within the next two days

As much as the last petrol protest was inconvenient, it certainly succeeded. And it could well do so again.

Of course, the bigger political picture is that this problem belongs to Mr Brown rather than Mr Blair - and it's not good for a leader-in-waiting to be seen in a bad light… Could Mr Blair use this crisis to his advantage, and prevent (or at least make more difficult) the passing of the mantle to Mr Brown? I doubt it, but it's certainly a possibility.

/ Posted 10th September 2005

Gordon's rainbow budget

Gordon Brown today announced the detail of his tenth, and final, budget. It has an environmentally green donation to African rainforests, a Labour-red increase in spending on schools and hospitals, a Tory-blue tax cut, and probably something Lib Dem-yellow in there too. Frankly, I got too bored wading through it to notice.

It's the all-things-to-all-men budget. It sticks up for the little guy by cutting income tax, then screws them over to reward big business by increasing tax rates on small companies while cutting corporation tax. It tries to be green by increasing tax on the biggest gas guzzling cars, but then restricts itself to *only* the biggest gas guzzling cars. It claims to simplify the tax system by cutting the 10% rate on income tax - but confuses everybody by keeping it for savings income.

Perhaps the main message from the budget comes from all of the ensuing media coverage - nobody quite knows whether they'll be better off or not, because this Chancellor has created a tax system so complex that it's impossible for any human to get to grips with the changes right away. Yet he still gets his headline tax cuts, despite the fact that it's likely many people will be *worse* off. So everyone loves him while also being screwed over by him.

It's headline-driven sound-bite government. And they said Gordon Brown was different…

/ Posted 22nd March 2007

The Conservative Party

The Conservative Party were humiliatingly defeated in the 2005 General Election, despite making gains on polling day. However, the party has been reinvented under David Cameron, and it seems that their fortunes are beginning to change.

Conservative MP defects to Labour

Robert Jackson, a Conservative MP and former minister has crossed the floor and defected to the Labour Party. I think that it's rather unfortunate that MPs are allowed to do this. They get elected with the backing of one party, using their policies to convince the electorate to vote for them, and once they've got their seat they defect to another party with opposing views. It really isn't on.

Surely Mr Jackson knew back in 2001 that the Conservatives were drifting further rightwards - so why did he stand as their candidate? Perhaps because the local electorate are likely to vote Conservative? Since he's standing down at the next election, and hence doesn't need to seek re-election, this seems a likely reason.

Perhaps there's a tactic for some of the minor parties here - get their supporters to join one of the big parties for which people are likely to vote, and once elected, switch to the minority party, thereby getting them seats in the Commons that they probably would not otherwise have gained.

Therefore, I feel that the most honest thing for Mr Jackson to do in these circumstances would be to resign as a Conservative MP, triggering a by-election in which he should re-stand as a Labour MP, giving the electorate a representative with whose party line they agree. But he wouldn't want to do that, because he might be defeated.

The BBC says that he believes students should pay tuition fees, that Tony Blair should not be criticised over his handling of the Iraq war and that more power should be given to Europe.

How long has he believed all this? If he's believed it since before 2001, then I hope he didn't campaign against his beliefs, as this would make him a very dishonourable and dishonest Member. Perfect for the Labour party, then.

/ Posted 16th January 2005

Howard raises fears of race riots

Last week, things were beginning to look good for Mr Howard. He was looking good, making sensible pledges, and Labour was in self-destruct mode. If only he'd continued in that style, he could easily have made a significant dint in the election results.

And then he goes and announces an utterly ridiculous set of policies on asylum and immigration, introducing arbitrary quotas. He's seems to have gone into self-destruct mode. I don't know who he's trying to appeal to with this announcement (other than the winner of ITV's *Vote for Me*), but these terrible proposals are just draconian and unnecessary. There's nothing logical about quotas. As the Guardian reports today:

> A quota would also be slapped on how many refugee seekers Britain is prepared to take, and once the limit was reached even those with genuine claims of persecution would be rejected.

With everything that is going on in the world, Mr Howard wants to turn the genuinely desperate away from Britain's door. That isn't just bad electioneering, it's just wrong.

> The Tory leader's decision to go on the offensive over asylum and immigration - with a newspaper advert today listing his beliefs about immigration, claiming that Britain has 'reached a turning point' and only his party has the 'courage to act' - will inevitably bring charges of playing the race card.

There's no need to 'accuse' Mr Howard of playing a race card here. He's effectively saying 'I don't want so many foreigners in our country'. And it's a sick thing to say. Particularly for the son of Romanian immigrants.

And if he's trying to reach the Daily Mail readers, I think he'll find that they have a new minority group to incite hatred against of late: Gypsies.

Making people apply for asylum from their home countries is one of the most ludicrous suggestions I've heard from Mr Howard. Just imagine that there are people coming after you, trying to kill you, and you genuinely fear that you're not going to see another day. No longer will you be able to fly to England, and be assured of help in your time of desperation. Instead, you are expected to sit in your home and fill in forms, send them off, and wait for a response. That just is not practical in the situation.

I understand that it can be perceived that there is a problem with immigration in this country, with the rate being rather higher than the ideal. I'm not a great believer in this. I think that the main problem with immigration and asylum in this country is that we don't help the people seeking immigration or asylum enough, so they end up feeling isolated and not a part of the community. If Mr Howard wants to restrict immigration slightly in order than more GBP per person can be spent on extra help for these people, then I think that this could be a positive move. But I'm more confident that Mr Howard proposes to use the 'savings' from this policy to cut tax.

Quotas on asylum are definitely not the answer. If Michael Howard genuinely believes there is a problem with the number of new citizens entering our country (a problem which I'm not convinced exists at the moment), then by all means restrict immigration if you must, but please don't stop helping genuine refugees.

/ *Posted 23rd January 2005*

Tories plan HIV tests for migrants

I thought I should set out why I am against the recently announced Tory plans to test the health of migrants before they enter the country. On the one hand, it would clearly reduce the burden on the NHS, which is largely a good thing. But at what cost?

Combined with the other proposals put forward by the Conservatives, it risks creating an immigrant under-class. If we are only to take a given quota of the best skilled and most healthy specimens, it begins to sound like these people are being treated as nothing more than commodities. This can't really do much to help social integration.

A TV story on the Labour response to the proposal claims:

> Labour rubbished Michael Howard's plans for HIV checks on immigrants this morning, calling them 'untested, uncosted and chaotic'.

This just makes the government look silly. Clearly, any proposal when it is first put forward is untested. So that's an unfair allegation. It's only uncosted because the government have failed to keep an accurate check on the health of immigrants to this point in time. And how can anybody claim that the system, which has yet to be implemented, will be 'chaotic'? I think Des Browne must just have been a bit desperate for a word to finish his pattern of three, there.

The Lib Dems, in the form of Mark Oaten, have come flying to the rescue with some sensible and wise words:

> Their shadow home secretary, Mark Oaten, said: 'This is another worrying step in the war of words over asylum and immigration between Labour and the Conservatives.
>
> 'They are in danger of pandering to prejudice rather than challenging it.'

It's beginning to become a consistent pattern here that I'm favouring Lib Dem policies. But I don't particularly want to be taxed to death once I'm earning, and I should (hopefully) qualify under the next government.

It's an interesting puzzle, but if I were judging purely on today's announcements, I'd have to vote Lib Dem, as they are the only party who have spoken with any degree of common sense.

/ Posted 15th February 2005

Conservative leadership 'race'

Ken Clarke's hopes of becoming the Conservative leader have been dashed this evening, as he's been knocked out of the Tory leadership race (I'm using the word 'race' in the loosest possible sense). That's a good thing, because he's not someone to whom I've ever particularly warmed. But then, frankly, I'm not that fussed about the other three either. Clearly none of them seem strong enough to be PM, and to be honest none of them even strike me as a particularly good leader of the opposition… So when David Cameron wins it, don't be surprised if I'm rather critical for a change.

But the best part about this story is Ken's comment:

> I think it sends a message that they are looking for a younger leader probably, but I don't think my age was remarkably relevant

Translated: *Err, I didn't win cos they want a young bloke innit, but, I dint do nuffink gov, the fact I ain't young had nuffink to do wiv it*

Condensed: *Yeah, but no, but yeah*

/ Posted 18th October 2005

And the winner is… David

As the Conservative leadership content heats up to an almost tepid finale, it's becoming increasingly obvious that the next General Election will be fought between Gordon Brown and David. But which David? Well, Cameron, most probably. Let's be realistic here. The chances of David Davis winning are, frankly, low. This represents an interesting moment in modern politics - the heavyweight, overbearing Labourite vs the touchy-feely everyman Conservative. Reverse the party allegiances, and that could've been written ten years ago. Well, maybe not. John Major was never exactly heavyweight or overbearing, but he was clearly very 'establishment', something of which Brown also has a flavour.

My point (if I have one) is that the electorate appear to be looking for a change in leadership style, and bizarrely it's Labour who are likely to supply this, while the Conservatives are desperately trying to emulate Blair. Which is somewhat unusual, and seemingly unwise.

But perhaps the Conservatives aren't going for the Blairite approach at all. Perhaps they're actually trying on the 'chat-show Charlie' Lib Dem approach, given that Charlie Kennedy is seemingly the most liked of the party leaders. If Cameron can manage to turn the Conservatives into something resembling a modern party, where a wide range of views are held, openly discussed, and considered, instead of the Labour approach of everybody being whipped into Tone-clones, then maybe he'll be very successful. But then, when the Conservative party get talking, they seem to suddenly discover that they really don't like each other, and re-enter the wilderness years where a number of factions roughly equal to the number of Conservative MPs appear, and no-one quite knows what's going on, or what the party stand for, but are united in their dislike for the current leader. And the next leader. And possibly the one after that, too.

It seems rather cruel to criticise Cameron before he's even taken office. But heck, since when has that stopped me? At the end of the day, in all likelihood he'll do a reasonably good job. But without the united support of the party, that'll mean nothing.

/ Posted 4th December 2005

Conservatives top latest poll with 42%

An interesting poll to be published in the Guardian later today reveals that in a contest between Cameron, Blair, and Campbell, the Conservatives would come out with 42% of the vote to Labour's 29% (and the Lib Dems' 17%). They then go on to say how this is the Conservatives best rating since just after they won the 1993 General Election, and Tory bloggers like Iain Dale get quite excited about this - and understandably so.

Except, it's not *quite* true. That is, it isn't really a genuine poll rating in the strictest sense, because it's asking about a hypothetical situation using a completely different question to the standard ICM polling question, which makes comparison somewhat nonsensical. Admittedly, the Conservatives have gained on the state of play garnered via the same question last month, but I'm not a great believer in the question in the first place. It's asking people to compare two relatively established leaders with one that's sort of in a No-Man's-Land: Of course the established visionary will come out on top over somebody who's not really had a great chance to state his case fully in front of the nation. And spin as required.

Iain Dale reckons a couple more polls like this will get Labour MPs 'twitchy' about Mr Brown's potential performance. I tend to disagree. I think Mr Brown needs a good crack of the whip before he'll improve poll ratings, and if the only realistic alternative is John Reid… well, I think the country's better off with Brown.

Looking at the more interesting data - the standard three-party comparison - the Tories are still doing well. They're on 40%, to Labour's 31%. But, of course, that's still a slightly sticky comparison, as the current situation doesn't reflect that at the next General Election. Essentially, what I'm saying is that polls taken right now don't mean an awful lot, and probably shouldn't be leading national newspapers.

That said, general trends are always of interest, and the Conservatives have been in the lead for almost a year now. *That's* significant. The trends are showing that the Conservatives are taking a real hold of support, and their grip is gradually tightening. Of course, our slightly perverse electoral system means that they'll need to keep that grip rather vice-like to actual turn it into a Parliamentary majority come election time, but perhaps that's possible.

I would say that this poll should certainly stop Mr Cameron from crying in his cornflakes tomorrow morning, but it really shouldn't be a champagne breakfast. He appears to be doing well - though it's difficult to tell quite *how* well - but there's an awful long way to go yet. Let's hope he keeps fighting.

/ Posted 20th February 2007

The Liberal Democrat Party

The Liberal Democrat Party made large gains in the 2005 General Election, and were really the only party who could claim a true victory. However, thanks to party infighting more characteristic of the bigger two, they have largely failed to capitalise on this position.

'No glass ceiling' on poll ambitions, says Kennedy

And lo, the battle was joined. Well, not quite - the election date still hasn't been announced, but the Lib Dems have entered the election fray and joined the party, bringing their own slogan along for laughs:

> The Real Opposition

Not the best slogan, I suggest, for a party which claims to have its sights set on Number Ten, but a decent one for a party who think they have a chance of becoming the official opposition. Or, at least, holding the balance of power. And heck, it's an awful lot better 'Britain forward not back' (I still don't know what that means), and 'Less talk, more action' (our problem is that Tony Blair's gone too far and taken too much action, like invading Iraq).

But there's nothing in Charles Kennedy's speech that I can vehemently disagree with. I'm not a massive fan of his tax policies, but at least he's *honest* about raising the top rate, and at least he has rational, good reasons for doing so.

The problem with the Liberal Democrats is that their greatest strength is also their greatest weakness:

> For us politics isn't about gimmicky pledge cards with vacuous statements. It's about real solutions to real problems. It's about being straightforward about how you will deliver. And it's about being straightforward also about how much it will all cost.

In this world of instant news, people need hooks and quick, meaningless soundbites, slogans, and pledges. That's the nature of the country we live in. Politics should be about much more, but people aren't interested enough to sit and listen to a reasoned argument - they want to be drip-fed what they want to hear. But once a party starts to subscribe to this form of argument, they lose all credibility.

The Lib Dems are still looking like the party I'm most likely to vote for, not least because we have similar opinions, but also because the other two main parties are just unsupportable in my view: Labour, because they are dishonest and spin to the point of lying in order to massage their egos, and The Conservatives because I can't support their despicable asylum policies, which border on racism.

I don't think the Lib Dems have a hope of winning the next election, but that shouldn't stop anybody voting for them. The bigger their majority, the louder their voice of reason. And if there's one thing we need in the House of Commons, it's more reasonable, moral people.

/ Posted 5th March 2005

Kennedy assassinated

Charles Kennedy, the most successful leader of the Liberal Democrats in many years, has been forced by his own MPs to resign as party leader, despite huge support by the party at large, and huge public support.

Charles admitted earlier in the week that he had openly and repeatedly lied about having a drinking problem. He called a leadership election so that the party membership could decide whether or not he should continue as their leader, and yet a cabal of MPs decided that the membership might make the 'wrong' decision, and so chose to announce that they wouldn't serve under Kennedy, forcing him into resignation.

This is a great achievement by these rebel MPs: They've destroyed their most successful leader, split the party down the middle, alienated the party membership, and left the Lib Dems in turmoil going into the May elections. There can hardly be a more destructive thing to do, particularly when we're seeing the Conservatives reviving and moving more towards the middle-ground which has traditionally been Lib Dem territory. And, just when David Cameron is repositioning his party as the different party avoiding 'Punch-and-Judy politics', the Lib Dems have successfully positioned themselves as the same back-stabbing, puerile idiots which turn the public off. Well done.

Having said all that, it was clear that Charles couldn't continue as leader. Except in the world of *The West Wing*, you can't openly lie about a serious medical problem, especially during an election campaign, and not expect it to come and destroy you at some point in the future. But would it really have been too difficult to convince him in private to resign, and hence avoid all of this mess and a big party split? There must have been a better way to deal with this: After all, it can't have been handled much worse.

Even his resignation announcement has been badly handled. His statement, critical of the Parliamentary party, will now run in the Sundays, and again in the Mondays. That's two days of Lib Dem bashing where it could have been just one had he announced yesterday or tomorrow. Whoops.

Who will replace him? Well, to be perfectly honest, there don't seem any particularly startling candidates that spring to mind immediately. But then, Kennedy didn't seem startling. He was the different, down-to-Earth 'nice-guy' of politics, which is what made him so popular in the party and in the country. We can only hope that his successor will be as popular, or the still-progressing era of three party politics will go into serious regression.

/ Posted 7th January 2006

Mark Oaten resigns

Mark Oaten has been forced to resign as the Lib Dem Home Affairs Spokesman, as he has some, erm, Home Affairs of his own to take care of, after some Away-from-Home Affairs to be reported in tomorrow's *News of the World.*

The 41-year-old father of two allegedly had an affair with a 23-year-old rent boy. If you're going to screw up your career, I guess you should do it in style - and a homosexual affair with someone half your age is about as far as one can credibly go, I guess.

Some will no doubt claim that it's unfair he's had to resign over something which says nothing about his professional competence, and I have some sympathy with that point of view. But it's just not a realistic stance to take in today's society, sadly. He had to resign, because he would never be allowed to talk about the issues.

More surprising is that he gave a classic non-apology in his statement, of the type perfected by New Labour:

> I would like to apologise for errors of judgement in personal behaviour and for the embarrassment caused, firstly to my family but also to my friends, my constituents and my party.

He apologises for errors in judgement - that is, getting caught - and the embarrassment it caused, but not actually for the incident itself. Which is surprising, because I thought he'd be the kind of guy to give a grovelling apology practically for being born. But then, I guess he'd have had to resign as an MP as well if he'd gone down that route, so perhaps it's not so surprising.

On something of a sidenote, it's been an amazing couple of weeks for the *News of the World* - Sven allegations last week, more promised this week, a journalist in the Palace, and Oaten allegations this week. Certainly not bad going on their part.

One Springeresque final thought on Mr Oaten: His website hasn't been updated yet. It says:

> It's been an eventful past couple of weeks ... I'm looking forward to a quiet weekend with my family before making any decisions on what the future may hold.

Somehow, I doubt he got his wish.

/ Posted 21st January 2006

Mark Oaten produces the best excuse ever

For the best part of the last academic year, some friends and I have had a running joke that the best excuse ever is, 'I'm sorry, I can't do that, I've shit myself' (due credit to Guardian columnist Charlie Brooker). It really works in any given situation. However, I've found a new pretender to the crown.

You may remember that one of the most esteemed weekly news journals of our time - the *News of the World* - found that Mark Oaten MP, a dedicated husband and father, had been having a relationship with a rent boy. Oopsie. But, according to the BBC today, he had a great excuse:

> In an article for the Sunday Times, Mr Oaten said his fall from grace was prompted by a mid-life crisis brought on by his rapid hair loss.

'I slept with a rent boy because my hair fell out'. It could be taken straight from the cover of *Chat* or *Pick Me Up*. I should know, I unashamedly read these magazines when they're lying about the hospital…

But the *real* question here: With a killer excuse like that, *why did he have to resign*? I can't imagine. But he obviously never consulted Prentiss McCabe. He should have said he was a fellow urban fox-spotter.

/ Posted 26th July 2006

Jute bags, green taxes, and Liberal Democrats

At this year's Liberal Democrat conference, delegates have been provided with environmentally friendly jute conference bags. They will be expected to use them again next year, rather than being issued with new ones.

But, reflecting a theme at this year's conference, the bag scheme has something of a hole. If the Lib Dems are serious about increasing their popularity, surely lots of new people will be at conference next year - without this year's jute bag. It's an idea that looks good in principle, but flaws are found with barely five seconds of armchair thought.

In this way, it's quite similar to "green taxes", which the Liberal Democrats have voted in favour of today. The first big test of Sir Campbell's leadership may have been passed with flying colours (passing a party motion about Green Taxes), but the first big test of logic is failed. Green taxes place the tax burden on polluting activities to discourage them. Yet the moment Green Taxes work, they fail: That is, the moment people are discouraged from polluting activities, there is no tax revenue for public services.

So, effectively, the Green Taxes either have to be stupidly low, so they don't discourage people, or stupidly high, so that a few pay a lot for a little pollution - which hardly fairly distributes the tax burden, since those who can't switch to expensive renewable energy sources (the lower socioeconomic classes) pay more. It's easy for CEO to buy a new non-polluting car, it's harder for Unemployed Joe who's driven the same old polluting banger for the last twenty-five years. If anything, it's the reverse of a LibDem policy.

/ Posted 19th September 2006

The British Political System

Sometimes, it's not the politicians I feel the need to moan about, but rather the imperfect political system practiced by the Mother of Parliaments.

The wife of the Prime Minister

Given the slightly silly way in which Mrs Blair has had to be included in the recent trip by the Prime Minister to the USA, with the two just 'co-incidentally' being in the US at the same time on different trips, and Mr Bush just 'happening' to invite her along, would it not seem logical to formalise the arrangements and have an official role for the Prime Minister's spouse, a role on which they could be elected alongside their husband rather than just happening into a job of such power?

Even the Prime Minister's Spokeswoman agrees with the general idea that Mrs Blair is an important stateswoman: After all, earlier today, when asked why Mrs Blair was introduced to the President by Her Majesty's Ambassador to Washington DC, she responded that this was normal for 'any prominent British citizen visiting Washington DC'.

I might be overanalysing this, but my dictionary defines prominent as 'conspicuous in position or importance'. As far as I am aware, Mrs Blair has no official elected position, and certainly no formal importance.

I have no ideological problem with the Prime Minister's spouse taking a bigger official role - I think that a First Lady style position could be very useful in some circumstances - and I think Mrs Blair is given an exceptionally bad press in this country for no good reason. But to take a bigger role means that they will no longer be able to hide behind the 'privacy of the family' excuse when things get tough. Mrs Blair simply cannot have it both ways: She cannot be both a stateswoman and also free from accountability. She has to take one with the other. And if she does, then good luck to her.

/ Posted 7th June 2005

Reform of the Parliament Act

The Parliament Act was designed to stop an elite band of Lords from preventing the passage of a bill favoured by the people. It is undeniable that the current Labour government have taken advantage of this, and forced through legislation that is at best controversial, and even potentially unpopular with the people, thanks to their huge Commons majority. It's clear, therefore, that an archaic law is being abused by a modern-day government to the potential detriment of the democratic process. Why, then, don't we reform this law?

We now live in an age where referenda are relatively easy to organise, especially if held alongside local elections. And when viewed in the context of the Act only having been used seven times in almost 100 years, it doesn't seem unreasonable to suggest that the Parliament Act should be reformed to suggest that the Commons can only overrule the Lords in the case where the Commons has the backing of the majority of voters in a referendum. In that way, the Act would truly be restricted to being used when the *people's* wishes are being ignored by the Lords, and would also prevent the abuse of the Act shown by the Labour government.

Obviously, urgent legislation couldn't be passed using these measures, but then it is highly unlikely that the Lords would have any wish to delay urgently necessary legislation anyway. This change would appear to give more power to the Lords, and perhaps slightly increase the obstinacy of the Chamber, invoking more use of the Act than at present; however, viewed on another level, it takes power away from the Commons and returns it to the people the Commons is supposed to represent. It's also possible that the piece of legislation being passed would be one that no-one really cared about, and so wouldn't really be motivated to cast a referendum vote upon, but again, that's unlikely as by the very nature of the process the legislation involved is likely to be controversial.

The final consideration is whether this would actually return power to the people, or increase the power of those in the media. Of course, in reality, it would probably do a bit of both - but we manage to get through General Elections every four years or so without worrying whether the votes are those of the people or those of media moguls, so I don't see why we can't manage the same in a referendum once every 13 years or so.

Overall, I think mine is a pretty good suggestion, even if I do say so myself. But I'm no expert, and I'm sure there's some major factor I must be overlooking. The future of the Parliament Act needs to be debated - so let's get on with it

/ Posted 7th November 2005

The trouble with Attorneys General

The Attorney General is a government appointee. He attends Cabinet Meetings, and is a very political figure. Indeed, Lord Goldsmith is a Labour peer.

Simultaneously, the Attorney General has supervisory powers over prosecution. He is the chief legal advisor of the Crown. He calls the legal shots in Britain.

Now, his two worlds have spectacularly collided, and this staunch Labour supporter is being asked to preside over the case of corruption within the Labour Party. If that's not a major conflict of interest, I'm not sure what is. Yet he refuses to step aside and 'butt out' of this affair, despite the fact that any fool can see that him being involved is not in the interests of true Justice being done.

The Government continues to use the slightly meaningless defence that 'it's always been that way' - well, yes, but never have we seen corruption to the heart of the governing Party quite like we have at the moment. It's a new situation, and as new situations arise our uncodified constitution is able to adapt - this is, and always has been, its great strength. Its great weakness is the virtually unchecked power handed to the Government of the day, and perhaps this is something that needs to be reformed in the world of corrupt politics.

Lord Goldsmith will be the last Attorney General of his kind. This situation has destroyed the credibility of the office. I'm not sure why, but that just *feels* like a significant blow in the downfall of the Labour Party: A 730 year old office falls apart because of the corruption of one small group of people.

I'm not sure whether to be depressed at the erosion, or to celebrate the wonderful versatility that this country's unique constitution provides. It's probably not for me to judge. But it seems worthy of a mention.

/ Posted 5th March 2007

The British Media

The British media are world renowned, but – much like our world renowned political system – they are often less than perfect. From unworthy stories getting acres of news coverage to questionable linguistic choices on news bulletins, I've covered many media stories. These are some of the best.

Teenagers not all rebels?

An amazing revelation from today's *Independent*:

> They enjoy quiet nights at home and view their parents as friends. Welcome to the world of today's "mild child" teenagers.

It turns out that not all teenagers are binge-drinking antisocial idiots, but that most are normal, reasonable human beings.

Perhaps someone should tell the *Daily Mail*, which prefers quotes like 'Teenagers [possess] pea-sized brains', 'Teenagers are mentally challenged' and 'Oral sex drive for teenagers' (all genuine). That's when it's not talking about teenage pregnancy, simultaneously criticising those who have abortions and those who choose not to have them and so become teenage parents. And they say Labour has no coherent policies on anything.

Oh, and just so you get a true flavour of this esteemed news journal, the current top story on their website is about David and Victoria Beckham's failure to smile whilst in St Mark's Square.

And they say we have the world's best newspapers.

/ *Posted 3rd May 2005*

Slow news day at the Daily Mail

I know editors have it tough when there's not much to report, but today's *Mail* is so unintentionally hilarious that I feel the urge to share it with you.

Page two has a large mug-shot of Richard Littlejohn (apparently not a recent one), and a report that he is rejoining the *Mail.* Somehow, they completely fail to mention that he's joining them from *The Sun*. Clearly, they don't want to be seen as a newspaper that accepts *The Sun*'s castoffs.

Then we have 'Complaints may force a change in the weather', a bit of a moan about the BBC's weather forecasts which contains no real news, and consists entirely of last week's articles on the same subject rehashed (even repeating the syndicated quote from Bill Giles, as if it is fresh). There's also a complaint about 'digitally generated rain' - so presumably they want us to go back to magnetic symbols.

Next, we learn that the word 'cost' has finally disappeared from the *Mail* lexicon, with the headline 'Delays that rip off customers to the tune of £370m will go, eventually'. Unfortunately, that particular headline is wrong on so many fronts as to be completely false, and contradicts the article completely. That's one subeditor that needs firing, then.

Then there's an article by some moaning teenagers who think they're hard done to because they go to private school, are predicted three A-Level 'A' grades, and yet have still been rejected by all their chosen universities. Apparently, they feel like they are being treated as second-class citizens. Have they not considered that A-Level grades aren't the only thing that is considered when applying to university? Frankly, if they moan as much as they do in this article, I wouldn't want them in my university either. One of them is a prospective medical student, who applied to three London colleges and Brighton and Sussex. Everyone who applies to study medicine at the London colleges has, at bare minimum, three 'A' grades. That's the very least you'd need. So to find he's been rejected should not come as a surprise, particularly as he's only studied two sciences. And he thinks people should be chosen purely on grades. Well that's probably exactly why he's been rejected.

Science reporter Robin Yapp files a report on ten questions that find whether you're blessed with that special charisma magic. Including, of course, the predictable picture of Diana.

There's a fascinating double-page spread on pop stars who look a bit like rock stars. Amazing. Oh, and then there's the equally amazing story of a small person who - get this - had a small flat! Hilarious! This is followed swiftly with another double-page spread about Jamie Oliver's wife's experiences of giving birth. How much did she get paid for that?

A 'leading doctor' - by which they mean someone who no-one's ever heard of who works in that world-famous Leicester hospital - suggests that parents should not be told the sex of their babies before they are born in case they decide to have an abortion based upon that knowledge. Except that's almost certainly not what he said.

'I had surgery to pin back my ears. Then one fell off.' You couldn't make these headlines up.

And the depressing thing is that I feel I've had to pick-and-choose from the ridiculous stories, otherwise I'd be sat here all day. So, if you want a laugh, go and buy today's *Mail.* Or check the website; current *top* story: 'I let my girl have sex at 11, admits mother'

/ Posted 25th May 2005

The media, terror fatigue, and bird 'flu

Just recently, the long-burning story of bird flu's potential to cause the due influenza pandemic has become almost daily front-page news, despite the fact that it's quite clear that any possible outbreak is months or even years away. Perhaps I'm being my usual over-cynical self, but could this not be symptomatic of the media tiring of terror, and Blair & Co. trying to distract the public from the disastrous anti-terror legislation they're trying to introduce? And if so, is that a problem?

Bird flu is pretty much the perfect story for the mass media. It's an unknown, almost intangible threat to life, which is widely predicted to be a big killer. It's indiscriminate, unfamiliar, and deadly. A bit like terrorism, but through a 'sexy' new sphere. And on top of all that, there's the requirement to decide who should get anti-viral drugs and vaccinations - meaning that the 'important' people have to be named, which plays on people's lingering sense of class division, one of the media's favourite British preserves.

As far as the government's concerned, it can quietly pass hugely controversial legislation whilst everybody else is distracted by the bird flu figures they're pumping out. The government also look very well prepared for the outbreak, and so get brownie points in that department, too. And, of course, they have lots of information they can drip-feed to the media, who will inevitably lap it up, as they expand their coverage of this 'inevitable disaster'.

In the worst-case scenario, there's a whole shed-load of questions for the media to be thinking about - if 50,000 die at home, but millions abroad, how does one lead the story? How do you balance accuracy, responsibility, and sensationalism, so as not to cause mass panic but also boost sales of *your* paper? I'm sure these questions will be addressed in the fullness of time, and for now, bird flu is a quick-and-easy unknown levelling enemy for the media - just what they like best.

So bird flu suits the government and suits the media for the moment, which is good news all-round. There looks to be no immediate end to this fascination too, with the spread of bird flu able to be tracked on a daily basis, and endless horror stories to print. But over time, it's inevitable that bird flu fatigue will set in, or some seminal event will give the news cycle a bit of a kick out of it's predictable cycle. And that's the worst part of the problem.

While bird flu will ungracefully fall from the front pages, the H5N1 virus will continue to mutate, the expected pandemic will be coming ever closer, and the pressure on the government to be proactive will be conversely shrinking. Of course, this might be fine, as the pandemic may be prevented by early action in the outbreak country - but there's always the slight possibility that it won't be, and that one of the biggest natural disasters of our time will be witnessed - we have to stay alert.

/ Posted 16th October 2005

Dixons to stop selling anything to anyone, ever

Ahh, Dixons. That famed electrical store which, three months ago, stopped existing as an actual entity, and turned entirely virtual with a woman poking at non-existing buttons on a non-existing screen and asking a non-existent customer 'When do you want it? … That's not a problem'. This was, of course, as parent company Currys ate up the Dixons brand and spat it out.

Dixons. What a marvellous shop it is. And ethically aware, too. It does lots of recycling - not least of press releases.

You may have seen in today's newspapers and news programmes that Dixons is to stop selling analogue radios, them being so old-hat. This news has had a mixed reaction on the web: Some are cynical, some think it's a step towards the future, some a sign of the times. But it's undeniably getting wide coverage. It must be nice for an electrical chain to get so much free advertising of it's modernity, but I can't be the only one for whom this story rouses a profound sense of *deja vu.*

It smells remarkably like a reheated story from last year, when Dixons decided to stop selling 35mm cameras, them being so old-fashioned and uncool. That, again, was seen as a big sea-change in consumer electronics, and generated much free advertising for the chain. But again, there was something not quite *fresh* about the story.

That might be because the year before, Dixons decided to stop selling video recorders, them being so old-school and obsolete. This generated much free advertising for the chain, and every talking-head worth their appearance-fee told us that this marked a huge shift the consumer electricals market. But some complained that this story might not have been quite as modern as they'd hoped.

Crazy suggestion, but that might just be due to the fact that a whole four months before, Dixons had decided to take a stand and stop selling Manhunt, a computer game which the parents of a murdered schoolboy blamed for his death.

'Ooh, look at our corporate responsibility for the modern age' cooed Dixons, to the sound of many press photographs outside their stores. Rumours that they later regretted this when stocks of the game completely sold out in the rest of the country due to massively increased demand thanks to the oxygen of publicity the case provided remain unconfirmed.

By now it must be struggling to think of things to stop selling. It apparently has personal CD players and 'boom boxes' on its 'endangered list', but if it's going to continue at this rate, there'll be no non-existent buttons left for the virtual Dixons woman to poke at.

It's hard to deny that Dixons have put out almost exactly the same story for *three years running* now, simply replacing one piece of technology for another, and yet it still generates acres of media coverage and free advertising. This either means that newspapers don't realise what Dixons are up to, or simply don't care about serving three-year-old reheated reports to their readers - after all, it fills another page in the lazy summer months.

/ *Posted 17th August 2006*

Suffolk murder victims: Women or prostitutes?

Currently, there appears to be much debate ongoing about the rights and wrongs of referring to the victims of the Suffolk murders as 'prostitutes'. Some argue that headlines should read 'Five women killed' rather than 'Five prostitutes killed', reasoning that the victims are first and foremost women.

I completely and utterly disagree.

Let us consider for a moment that the victims are not prostitutes, but bank managers. Five bank managers killed in the same area apparently in the same manner by what appears to be the same person. Almost certainly a targeted campaign against bank managers. What headline would you expect?

Why, then, should it be any different for prostitutes? Of course, it shouldn't. The only argument against using the term is that, to some, it appears judgemental and pejorative. Bollocks. It is merely an accurate description of their job, which (to me at least) confers no judgement.

The alternative being bandied about is 'sex worker'. This is so non-specific and outrageously euphemistic as to be insulting, suggesting that society is ashamed of these people and what they did for a living. Note, also, that the majority of prostitutes appear to prefer the term 'prostitute', and it appears in the name of 'The English Collective of Prostitutes', their organisation.

And why on Earth would we refer to them as 'women' in headlines? This merely picks out one characteristic, not particularly specific, that unites all of the victims, suggesting that the fact that 'young women' were murdered is far worse than murders of 'young men'. *That* is insulting.

Now, just to be clear, in the everyday context, these women are not defined by their jobs any more than anyone else. That is not my point. But when the most specific link of all the victims is their occupation, and it seems likely that it is intimately linked with their death, why bumble about avoiding the issue? They may have been beautiful young women with promising young lives, but they are undoubtedly united by the fact that they were prostitutes.

People need to get over their prejudices, and accept that 'prostitute' is a non-judgemental statement of specific fact. If they feel that it confers judgement, then perhaps, just perhaps, it is them doing the judging.

/ Posted 20th December 2006

Iran, the Navy, and BBC News 24

It strikes me as interesting today that *BBC News 24* is referring to Iran's detention of 15 Royal Navy personnel as a 'kidnapping', which seems to me to be extremely loaded language.

Iran contests that the boats involved in the incident were in Iranian waters, while the UK and US state that they were within Iraqi territory, so it appears one word against another. If the Iranians are right (and it is very hard to tell in such disputed territory with complex divisions), then they are well within their legal rights to detain the Royal Navy personnel, so to describe them as "kidnapped" in this rather less-than-clear situation seems unfortunate at best.

Most other news organisations - including the BBC's own website - are using diplomatic terms like 'seized' or 'detained' which, in themselves, do not imply that either side is right. So why is *BBC News 24* deliberately choosing to do differently? I hope, not least for the renowned journalistic standards of the Beeb, that this wasn't a decision taken because 'kidnapped' fits better on a headline graphic.

Some of their presentation decisions are already irritating and somewhat questionable, but if presentation is the reason for this decision, then standards really have reached a new - very depressing - low.

/ Posted 25th March 2007

The medium is not the message

There's been much comment recently about politicians reaching out to the 'yoof' vote through sites like YouTube, and Labour's embarrassing efforts thereon. Why is it that politicians believe that they can reach a politically disaffected youth by doing old things via new media? The problem isn't that teenagers don't want to see a speech by Tony Blair on TV, it's that they don't want to see a speech by Tony Blair. Sticking it on YouTube doesn't help.

It's a lot like Blair's idea to woo the MTV generation by appearing on, erm, MTV. That, too, was a bizarre idea. People watch MTV for *The Osbournes*, not for a party political broadcast. The medium is unimportant - if *The Osbournes* was broadcast via YouTube, it would be as popular as it was on MTV. A party political broadcast is as unappealing on YouTube as it is on the BBC. It isn't the medium politicians are getting wrong, and trying to hijack a medium won't get far.

The (relative) success of WebCameron comes from the fact that it does things differently. It allows users to post videos essentially mocking David Cameron and the Conservatives without complaint. It engages (albeit somewhat reluctantly) with the blogosphere's proclivity for awkward questions. In short, it allows people to disagree, mock the site and the system, and hence engage in something resembling a two-way conversation (however staged and controlled it is in reality).

That's why Labour, who are stuck in the Blairite era of tight media control can't hack it. They fear nothing more than discussion, debate, and a news cycle with a life of its own. So they can't engage with a youth currently obsessed by the idea of the democratisation of the media. Prepared speeches and crafted videos have no place and hold no interest for this youth, whether on YouTube, their iPod, or the BBC.

One of the great historical strengths of British politics has been the administration's ability to do almost anything it likes for four or five years, after which they will be judged by the electorate. As the electorate becomes more connected, and the sharing of ideas takes hold, then we enter a new form of democracy, where politicians are judged constantly, and opinions are constantly formed and reformed.

And *that's* the real message. People want to be heard, consulted, and involved - through any and all media. The political game has reached a tipping point, and however you disguise old-style politics, it just won't cut it in the brave new world.

/ Posted 23rd April 2007

Education, Education, Education

In 1997, Tony Blair announced that his three main political priorities were 'Education, education, education'. But has his government lived up to this promise? I've spent four years trying to decide for myself. These are some of my thoughts.

'Junk food' to be banned in schools

Ruth Kelly, the government minister determined to introduce *something* eponymous during her tenure, is apparently to ban junk food in schools. My question is: How?

Many schools are locked into implausibly long contracts with suppliers, from both catering and vending machine companies. These contracts include a great financial disincentive to early ending. So where's the money coming from to end these contracts by September 2006? Or does the government plan to do something quite sneaky, like change the law to make it illegal to supply such items in schools, and hence make any company doing so a law-breaker? It's an interesting idea, but it's hardly true to Labour values.

Or is Kelly just going to leave the ending of the contracts as each individual school's problem, possibly meaning that many will get into financial difficulty, and, by definition, all will have less to spend on education?

Or, in typical New Labour style, is this a well spun fudge? Kelly actually said…

> So today I can announce that we will ban poor quality processed bangers and burgers being served in schools from next September.

It would therefore appear that *good* quality processed bangers and burgers will be fine. And which company is really ever going to admit to selling 'poor' quality ones? And how is this 'quality' going to be regulated and judged?

On the subject of vending machines, the words falling out of Kelly's mouth were actually…

> And because children need healthy options throughout the school day I can also announce that from next September no school will be able to have vending machines selling crisps, chocolates, or sugary fizzy drinks.

It's noticeable, particularly on the fizzy drinks front, that most ranges have now switched over to production with 'no added sugar' - so presumably they don't count as 'sugary fizzy drinks', and therefore no change is needed. The statement about crisps and chocolates clearly doesn't rule out all sweets, biscuits, and similarly unhealthy snacks. And, of course, school 'tuck shops' will still be able to sell all of these things - because they are not vending machines.

Perhaps I'm just being overly cynical, but it appears to me that Kelly has announced a headline-grabbing policy of precious little substance. How very New Labour.

/ Posted 28th September 2005

Dyslexia: A myth?

Some ill-defined 'experts' have put their thinking caps on and come up with the hypothesis that dyslexia 'does not exist and is no more than an emotional construct'. Their full arguments will be put forward in a Channel 4 documentary next week, but there's an outline of them in today's Guardian. Now it's clearly foolish to comment on their theories before hearing them in full, but heck, I'm going to do so anyway.

I am by no means an expert in dyslexia, and I have very little experience with it. So frankly, I'm quite probably spouting ill-informed rubbish. But I don't think dyslexia is a myth. I think it's a genuine disorder which requires special treatment for those who suffer from it. I think there's a wealth of neurological and genetic evidence to suggest that such a condition exists, and to say it is merely a myth doesn't seem helpful or sensible. However, I think it's chronically over-diagnosed, and not nearly as widespread as it appears to be. As the producer of the aforementioned documentary puts it:

> Dyslexia persists as a construct largely because it serves an emotional, not scientific, function. Forget about letter reversals, clumsiness, inconsistent hand preference and poor memory - these are commonly found in people without reading difficulties, and in poor readers not considered to be dyslexic ... Public perceptions often link reading difficulties with intelligence and, in our culture, an attribution of low intelligence often results in feelings of shame and humiliation.
>
> It is hardly surprising, therefore, that the widespread, yet wholly erroneous, belief that dyslexics are intellectually bright but poor

> readers would create a strong, sometimes impassioned demand to be accorded a dyslexic label.
>
> Of course, some children will require special resources and dispensations, but we certainly don't need spurious diagnoses of dyslexia to achieve such ends.

The diagnosis of dyslexia essentially creates an excuse for poor reading, and can be used to garner extra support - both educational and emotional - for the child. For any child who is having difficulty at school, this diagnosis can provide the extra help they need, and so be seen as a very positive thing. It is also practically impossible to obtain an educational statement of needs - as well as the appropriate funding for the school - without some kind of medical diagnosis, and dyslexia provides the perfect solution. The statementing process largely fails to recognise that some pupils need individual support not because of a medical problem, but just because of a generalised learning difficulty - and without a statement, there's no money, and so no additional support, which means the child's performance is below par and hence the school's league table position slips.

There is, therefore, a practical incentive for the child to be diagnosed, and a financial incentive for the school which is conducted the testing to make the diagnosis. In such circumstances, it would be a minor miracle if only those with the condition were labelled as having it.

Of course, all of this does not mean that those incorrectly diagnosed with dyslexia are not genuinely struggling, and do not require extra help. But surely the over-diagnosis can only have a negative impact for the help given to those with dyslexia, as the evidential base for the help given becomes muddied by successes garnered from those without the condition.

As far as I can see, what's needed here is a greater recognition of generalised learning difficulties, so that each child can get the support they truly need without having to be wrongly burdened with a medical label for the rest of their life.

/ Posted 3rd September 2005

Money matters: Doctors vs Teachers

On *Guardian Unlimited*, Peter Preston has posed the controversial question: 'Is one doctor with three teachers?'

His article is interesting, and makes some good points about the fact that doctors should, perhaps, not complain about a pay increase when they are already far more highly paid than equivalent doctors in other European countries.

Unfortunately, his question is not so good: This is a comparison based on the latest doctors' contract, comparing consultants - the most highly paid doctors - with the average teacher. As a contrast, here's an alternative view.

A newly qualified teacher has an average debt of £12,069. Under the latest pilot scheme, the government repays this off for them as long as they work in teaching. They are paid an average of around £22,000, plus a £5,000 bonus for sticking it out for a year. That's £27,000. According to the Government, primary teachers work an average 39 weeks per year (38 teaching weeks, 1 admin/training week), at 37.5hrs per week (9-4.30, Mon-Fri). So they get roughly £18.46 per hour.

A newly qualified doctor has an average student debt of £15,000. Since the government doesn't understand that working nine to five every day precludes you from doing as much part time work as being at university for fewer hours, the average student has to supplement this with £5,000 of bank loans. That adds up to a first-year repayment of £467 worth of student debts, and £538 to the bank. The starting salary for a junior doctor is £20,295. Net income (before tax): £19,290. That's for the basic 47 weeks, at 45hrs per week (Mon-Fri, 9-6) plus variable overtime, which for argument's sake we won't include. That works out at £9.12 per hour: Just under half of what the teacher gets.

So, is one teacher worth two doctors? Or are questions like this conceptually flawed and misleading?

/ Posted 30th March 2006

National shock as 75% fail A-Levels

It's the story we never hear in the media. 75% of 18-year-olds have just failed to get three passes (grade E or above) at A-Level. Popular opinion, mainly thanks to the media, has it that over 80% of 18-year-olds reach this standard. Bollocks. The vast, vast majority of the young people in our country don't even attempt A-Levels, let alone pass them.

Let's talk, me and you, about one of the most respected, classical subjects at A-Level: History. Of the 375,000 18-year-olds in the country, the top 13% sat an A-Level in the subject. Frankly, that's an achievement. Schools no longer enter people they don't think will do well, because it damages their league table results and ultimately affects funding, which is why 87% of the population don't get to take it. So it is fair to say that the 13% of youngsters *sitting* the History A-Level are the top historians of their age in the land. Well done.

10.9% of the 18-year-olds in this country passed that A-Level. We've weeded out 89.1% of the population - hundreds of thousands of people - without even looking at grades. But if we choose to look at that top 'A' grade, we find that just 2% of the population managed to achieve it. 98% didn't.

In chemistry, only 9% of the population passed, with under 2% achieving the top grade. For maths, the top 13% were entered, and the top 3% got A's. And for the much lamented media studies, 7% were entered and just 1.5% got A's.

People say that A-Levels are easy, worthless, and don't discriminate anymore. Yet the vast majority don't pass them, and our example shows that very few reach the top grades. How much more discriminating would you like them to be?

/ Posted 18th August 2006

Health and the NHS

I am currently training to be a doctor, and so health issues and the state of the NHS tend to feature quite prominently in my writing. On the more controversial health topics, I tend to have quite detailed and strong opinions, and it is these which feature first in this chapter.

Voluntary euthanasia

A couple of days ago, the Head of Communications at the Voluntary Euthanasia Society (VES) sent me an email asking me to reconsider my position on voluntary euthanasia in the light of three recently published documents: Lord Joffe's Bill on Assisted Dying, a select committee report, and the most recent report into the way in which Oregon's system works.

All I've previously written on this site with respect to my views on euthanasia is the following brief comment:

> Whilst I agree with euthanasia in principle, I've yet to hear of a workable way for it to be put into practice and not be open to abuse. Therefore, I cannot support legislation legalising voluntary euthanasia.

Now, I've read the bill, I've glanced at the Oregon report (but admittedly not studied it), and, most clearly, looked at the handy flow chart provided by the VES. And I still have my concerns about it, and still wouldn't be able to support this particular bill. Here, I will explain some, but not all, of my reasons behind this decision.

My first, and possibly greatest, concern is that doctors will be asked to play an active role in killing someone, be this through supplying them with the medication to do so or actually administering it when the patient is unable to do so. This changes the job of the doctor, if not in a legal sense then certainly in a moral sense. I see the role of a doctor in the traditional 'first do no harm' sense, and to ask doctors to actively kill patients changes that perception utterly.

The situation reminds me somewhat of the often-quoted ethical case of the man who wants his left-leg amputated because he believes he has sinned and that God wants him to pay for these sins with his leg. Despite the man's clear request, and despite him having reasons which appear valid - even crucial - to him, it is still unethical to amputate the man's leg, as it would do him harm with no particular medical benefit.

Clearly, there is something of a gulf between amputating the leg of a healthy man and helping a terminally ill patient to die with dignity, but the underlying ethical principle is not so different. I recognise, as the Hippocratic Oath states, 'that prolongation of life is not the only aim of healthcare', but I equally agree, as it also states, 'not [to] provide treatments that are … harmful'. We can then get into a philosophical argument as to whether the ending of someone's suffering is actually harmful or helpful, but I think the meaning of the Oath is quite clear.

Another reason not to trust doctors with this power is that they're notoriously bad at discussing death. Many patients who should have discussions about whether or not they want to be resuscitated don't have them, because we all find it difficult to sit down with a patient and say, 'Well, it looks like you're going to die. Shall we discuss it?'. And there is, as far as I can see, no provision in the bill for further education for doctors to overcome this difficulty, nor any procedure by which this topic will automatically be discussed with patients who are in this category. If the doctor doesn't bring this up, and there is no system of making patients more aware, then you effectively disenfranchise those patients who are not up-to-date on Department of Health policies and procedures.

It is also worrying that, as part of the declaration process, a solicitor of all people is asked to judge whether a patient is 'of sound mind'. What possible training does a solicitor have to recognise such attributes? The bill also states that the patient should 'understand' what the declaration means. What exactly is meant by the word 'understand'? Are they to be given an explanation of simply the outcome - that they die - or the process? And if the process is to be explained, to what level is the explanation to be given, and how is the understanding to be tested? In most cases, doctors make a judgement here, but when it is quite literally a matter of life and death, I wouldn't want to be the person responsible for giving the explanation, or indeed checking that the patient understands. The language is far too woolly.

Whilst I have these practical objections, I think it is a terrible scar on the conscience of our society that we force people in terrible pain to extend their suffering. The patient's right to death is as important as their right to life. My problem is simply that I can't see an effective way of putting this system into practice, as I'm not comfortable with the treatment being administered by doctors, yet cannot see who else would be a natural choice for performing the procedure. And I don't think it is right, on an issue as important as this, to go with a bill that's simply 'as good as we are going to get'. This bill needs to be looked at in much more detail, examined as with a microscope until every scintilla of doubt can be removed from the whole process. There's no room for 'no reasonable doubt' in a bill to do with certifying people to death - there must instead be an absence of all doubt. And until such a time as I feel that this has been done, I simply cannot support this bill.

/ Posted 27th May 2005

Smoking banned in pubs and clubs

MPs have voted to ban smoking in all pubs and clubs in England. This is a tough one for me, because I'm very much on the fence on this issue. But, for the record, I don't smoke, and I don't like people smoking around me. That just doesn't necessarily mean I want it banned.

As a soon-to-be healthcare professional, I should be jumping up and down at the prospect of people not smoking in pubs and clubs, and raving about how this legislation will save people's lives, and reduce the rate of lung cancer and other smoking-related diseases. But I have my reservations. Yes, this will undoubtedly stop some casual smokers from smoking, and possibly thereby stop other people who might start as casual smokers from ever starting. It will also protect staff from the effects of passive smoking. Some lives will inevitably be saved.

But what about the (stereotypical) poor household, where dad would wander down to the pub for a pint and a smoke each evening? Is he not now going to smoke more at home, and do more damage to his poor kid?

And what of the heavy smokers, who are those most at risk of disease? This legislation is unlikely to change their habits. And what of the little villiage pubs? Is the local PC really going to Plod round there and slap a fine on them for failing to ban smoking? Especially if PC Plod himself smokes, or the consolidation of police forces means that he's out of a job and the nearest police station is fifty miles away? Will the problem not increase in these 'underground' pubs, where more people are potentially at risk as the pub serves as the hub of the community, and people are in there more often than the trendy wine bar in the city?

On top of all of that, it's another government dictat, which are inevitably controversial, and shift the balance of power further away from the people who elected the government in the first place.

My argument throughout this saga has been that if pubs are brave (like Wetherspoons briefly was), then they'll ban smoking. If there's such a demand for non-smoking venues, then their business will increase, and other pubs will be economically forced to follow suit - including the little village pub, who would be introducing the change off their own back, and so be more inclined to make the ban stick. This would be a gradual change, which would change the public's and smokers' attitudes to smoking in general, and would probably have more far-reaching effects than simply banning smoking in these areas. Smoking would become increasingly socially unacceptable, which is a powerful force in getting people to give up.

So, whilst the ban is clearly a good thing in that it will save lives, I'm still not convinced that it was the *best* way to tackle the problem. But it's *a* way, and it looks like it's here to stay.

/ Posted 15th February 2006

Choosing our battles: Why fight HIV?

HIV and AIDS are terrible. They're particularly terrible if you're living in a country where anti-retrovirals are not available, and I don't want to appear to trivialise that. But worldwide, the bigger estimates state that only 38 million people have HIV. That's less than two-thirds of the UK population. Given that we have a very limited pot of money to tackle health problems in the developing world, is HIV the best thing to tackle?

Many people like to try and wage war with HIV on the basis that it's easy to prevent. It's said that practicing safe sex, or abstinence, prevents HIV infection. That's true. But that doesn't make it *easy* to tackle. Even in the most developed and scientific of nations, we can't get the safe sex message across. The UK has an appallingly high rate of teenage pregnancy, sexually transmitted infections, and sexually-transmitted HIV. Over 50,000 people in the UK are HIV positive, and that number is growing by almost 7,000 per year. We're much better placed to tackle HIV than are aid workers with limited resources in Africa, not least because this country has a much lesser objection to the use of barrier contraception. Tackling HIV is *not easy.*

Treating HIV is vastly expensive. Conservative estimates say that anti-retroviral treatments cost a minimum of US$3,600 per year. Providing anti-retrovirals does not *cure* HIV, it merely slows its progress. And looking at things in a cruelly scientific way, the longer an HIV positive person is alive, the greater the risk of infecting a greater number of people. I'm not condoning murder of all HIV positive people in Sub-Saharan Africa, and it's not an entirely sensible way of looking at things, but it's an opinion held by many.

On the other hand, malaria affects 500 million people per year, and is easily and cheaply preventable. Yet 20% of child deaths in Sub-Saharan Africa are due to malaria. A child dies every of malaria every thirty seconds. 95.2% of malaria infections can be prevented with a US$5 mosquito net impregnated with insecticide, which is effective for 5 years. In many test villages, malaria was eradicated by these nets. For the same cost as treating one person with HIV for one year, 720 nets can be bought. For the cost of the cheapest anti-retroviral treatment for every HIV suffer for a year, over *14 billion* of these nets could be bought - malaria could be virtually eradicated.

Malaria is, by no means, a death sentence. Treatment is cheap - US$0.90 for a child, US$2.40 for an adult. But with so many infections, the cost soon adds up. So to claim that malaria is not worth preventing because it's cheaply treatable is inaccurate, and makes little sense.

Malaria isn't as perversely marketable as HIV. It's not a taboo subject, and it gets little press because it affects the poorest of the poor, not the richer parts of African society. Think: When was the last time you heard the phrase 'Millions dying of HIV in Africa'? When was the last time you heard of 'Millions dying of malaria in Africa'? Fewer die of malaria than HIV, but it affects many more people, and we could feasibly eradicate malaria right here, right now. Why don't we?

People with HIV and the scores of other infections which kill Africans should not be left to die. We have to do something, and we have to start somewhere. Why not with malaria?

/ Posted 11th June 2006

Our children dying because of our embarrassment

The Observer reports today that a leaked report shows that the NHS is 'failing our children' through a lack of Child and Adolescent Mental Health Services (CAHMS). And how.

One quarter of the country does not have crisis teams for Child and Adolescent Mental Health Services. That is beyond belief. If the report was that we didn't have ambulances to pick up children in 25% of the country, nobody would accept it, because we know children would die. Newsflash: *The lack of crisis teams means children are dying.*

Imagine for a second that, god forbid, your child is standing on your roof and threatening to jump and kill himself. Who do you call? In 25% of the country, there's no-one to help. Imagine your teenager suddenly has horrific hallucinations of millions of spiders coming to kill him. In 25% of the country, there's no-one to help. Both of these children might kill themselves, because *in 25% of the country, there's no-one to help* - and all because we're pulling funding from such services to serve the less common but more palatable diseases like cancer.

We're awful at providing mental health services in general, because we don't like to talk about them. We like to imagine that the 'crazy' people are locked up, and brand every criminal going as having some mental health problem - usually schizophrenia - because we can't accept that some people do things that are wrong through logical choice. Mental health and criminality become inextricably linked, and who wants to spend money helping criminals?

This is an utterly ludicrous situation. 9 million people in this country - one in six - has a mental health disorder *right now*. More than 1 in 3 of us will have a mental health disorder at some point - more than will experience cancer. Yet we're *cutting* the amount spent on mental health services. Where's the logic?

The situation is worse for children, because as repulsive as society finds the idea of an adult with mental illness, the idea of a child with it is far worse. When was the last time some do-good charity collector asked you for money for children with cancer? And when the last time they asked you for money for children with mental health problems? The latter is *56 times more common*. Yet in some parts of the country, there are no Child and Adolescent Mental Health Services *at all*.

We need to get over ourselves and face these issues or our own children will continue to suffer. And there's a pretty big chance it will be your children next.

/ Posted 23rd July 2006

Why the NHS really spends too much on drugs

The OFT published a much journalised report earlier this week about how the NHS is spending far too much on branded drugs. It's a frustrating report, because they so *nearly* got to the point of the issue, but not quite.

Their problem is, effectively, that people are being prescribed branded drugs which are no more effective than non-branded generic versions. This is probably true in a minority of cases. But in many cases, the drug brand does make a difference. It shouldn't, but it does. Let me provide a couple of examples.

First, the technical one. There is a wealth of evidence that different brands of identical epilepsy drugs have different effects. The reasons are unknown - and, in a world of evidence based medicine where we *do* what works rather than *understanding* what works, they are likely to stay that way. So in this case, the spend on the branded drug may well be justified. This is one example that springs to mind, there are probably many others.

Secondly, the prosaic reason. Believe it or not, medicine in a person works better than medicine in a cupboard. Quite often, for their own bizarre reasons, patients won't take generic medications, but prescribe a branded version, and they're quite happy. This is, perhaps, more common in kids where there is a choice between the generic flavourless version and the branded flavoured version. If the medication is necessary, then it's necessary to get it into the patient. If that means prescribing a more expensive version because the patient is awkward, that's sometimes justifiable too.

But more than this, the overspend on drugs has little to do with branded drugs. They so nearly hit the mark when they said the system should be changed 'to deliver better value for money from NHS drug spend and to focus business investment on drugs that have the greatest benefits for patients'. So close, and yet so far.

You see, a great number of the drugs we pump into people have no effect. This isn't because doctors are cruel, it's because this is (or so it would seem) what the government wants. If your blood pressure is 139/89, you won't get pills. If your blood pressure is 140/90, you might well do. You're not at a hugely increased risk with an increase of 1mmHg, but the Government has decreed that patients above an arbitrary hypertension cut-off must receive treatment to prevent *some* of them developing future complications. There's very little judgement in this on the doctor's part - an untreated patient is a failure, even if the doctor's best judgement suggests they shouldn't be on treatment. And this story is repeated over countless conditions with countless protocols. We're spending money on drugs that even the doctor often feels are unnecessary.

There are a whole host of other areas in which the NHS overspends on drugs, too. Drugs which patient's use to decorate their kitchen cupboards; drugs which are on repeat prescription but never used; drugs prescribed 'because' a person has free prescriptions, which cost very over the counter; drugs prescribed (sometimes understandably) to get patients off doctors' backs.

Branded medications are the tip of a very large iceberg, much of which is controlled by a Government who insist on telling doctors what to prescribe, and to whom, rather than letting their years of clinical judgement be used to their full extent.

Perhaps one day, someone will actually get round to taking the NHS in hand, and righting the wrongs. Perhaps. But for the moment, it seems the powers that be are content to tinker around the edges of huge problems in a massively frustrating way, whilst avoiding the real issues and the difficult decisions. No politician wants to 're-educate' patients on the things they do wrong in their interactions with the NHS, because the punters are the voters. Nobody wants to look weak by admitting past failings and correcting them. Nobody wants to actually *fix* the problems.

But surely *someone* can see that the deckchairs have been re-arranged enough, and that HMS NHS needs some urgent righting? Or should I find myself a life-raft now?

/ Posted 20th February 2007

Reform of the Mental Health Act

Labour have long wanted to reform the Mental Health Act, and made their first attempt with the Mental Health Bill 2002, which failed rather spectacularly. Several further attempts have also proved fruitless. But now they're having an all-new attempt at reforming the Act.

Firstly, in true modern NHS style, it now means that the range of people empowered to do things is vastly extended. Where the power to detain people and force treatment upon them was previously restricted to a select few with the necessary skill and experience, the Government now wants to extend this power to a great many more people - in fact, pretty much anyone who claims to work with the Mental Health sector who's been on a short course. And it will be the Social Service - not medics - who decide if someone can be deemed to be an Approved Mental Health Professional.

This is nurse-prescribing gone mad. Of course, Mental Health nurses have long been highly trained in the detention of individuals for short periods, and they play a very important role in this arena. But now the government wants to open this up to *any* Mental Health professional. Dodgy counsellors will no medical training will soon be able to sign up for a course, then will be able to detain people. That sounds unhelpful to say the least.

Just to make it even easier for these poorly trained individuals to know who they can round up, the Government would like to change the definition of a Mental Disorder. Instead of detailed definitions of each kind of disorder, the Government now wants us to accept "any disorder or disability of the mind" as a definition. This is beyond stupidity. Now, anyone who has epilepsy or has suffered a stroke or has any number of conditions suddenly falls under the provisions of the Mental Health Act, and the mountains of bureaucracy that entails. I'm sure that'll come as a particular delight to overworked GPs, general physicians, and mental health workers nationwide.

And, ho-hum, they feel a need to better regulate these powers. So they're introducing much greater use of Mental Health Tribunals. Anyone who's ever tried to organise a Tribunal for a patient will know that it's damn-near impossible, so to use *more* of them seems - well, not a great idea.

Yet this stinking piece of terrible legislation is getting very little media coverage because of public embarrassment about Mental Health.

There is one glimmer of hope - It's hard to deny that most of the Cabinet have "disorders of the mind", so we can wait till they pass the new legislation, then lock the lot of 'em up. But by then, it will be too late.

/ Posted 14th March 2007

Criticism of Patientline costs

The Observer reports today that Patientline, a private company, is being accused of charging NHS patients exorbitant rates to use the phone and watch TV using bedside systems installed at the company's cost.

This is a private company which has paid to help improve NHS services. As with any private company, the most important thing for them is that they make money, and they've spent millions of pounds installing the Patientline service with the government's backing. Now that they are trying to recoup those costs, and make a profit, it is the private company that is being criticised.

This seems deeply illogical to me - the NHS is so mis-funded that private companies are having to be brought in provide the services which patients view as necessary. Patients are then asked to pay for these services, because the government won't. And yet it is the private company which gets criticised.

Michael Summers, chairman of the Patients Association, says: 'It's critical that people who are unable to visit a sick, elderly or very young patient should be able to get through to them at a reasonable price. These charges are too high and callers should be told very clearly how much they're paying for the service.'

Surely in a National Health Service, it is the job of the government to provide 'critical' services. Their failure to do so should reflect badly on them, not the private companies they invite to step into the breach. And I'm quite surprised that *The Observer* of all newspapers has chosen not to point this out.

/ Posted 24th July 2005

Divine answer to earthly question

Gideons International recently asked Leicester NHS Trust if it could put Bibles into patients' bedside lockers. The hospital responded that they would like some time to investigate whether or not there was a possibility that having the same Bible there for each occupant might pose an MRSA risk. To me, that seems a sensible request.

Iain Mair, executive director of Gideons International UK doesn't think it's sensible: 'They are saying there's a potential MRSA risk, and we say that is nonsense.'

I'm not sure what expertise Mr Mair has in the field of infection control, but I'm fairly convinced that he doesn't have quite the same qualifications as the Trust's Infection Control team. He claims that Gideons International has commissioned reports from consultants to disprove the theory. Surely there would be little point in commissioning such research if he is not then going to allow the Trust to examine the research prior to reaching a decision on the matter?

The tabloids have become (predictably) become angry about a 'hospital plan to ban Bibles' recently. Despite the fact that there is, as yet, no such plan. But that's not the kind of thing that's stopped them before. Other papers called it 'tantamount to banning the Bible from NHS wards'. That's obviously not true either.

The Leicester NHS Trust also wish to take time to consider whether allowing the provision of these Bibles would appear as the Trust favouring one religion over another, which seems a fair enough thing to consider. Unless you're Iain Mair, in which case: 'It's political correctness gone mad.'

It would clearly be impractical to have a whole library of religious books supplied to each patient. And yet, I wonder if Mr Mair would think it 'political correctness gone mad' if all patients were to be supplied with copies of the Koran, and, along with his plan, given advice that 'other religious texts are available'.

The Trust wants to investigate the possibility of tracking which patients have come into contact with which texts, so that potentially infectious ones could be removed from circulation. That seems fair, if something of an invasion of privacy. The best solution, as I see it, would be to make patients aware that religious texts were freely available to take away and take home. That way, the religious texts get further than just being something to read when you're bored in hospital, and the infection problem is essentially overcome.

I'm sure the Trust will come up with a solution that will be appropriate to all parties. Although, frankly, I'd be rather less inclined to help when Gideons International wants to make such a fuss over such a small issue. But that's probably just me.

/ Posted 5th June 2005

One of the most controversial areas of modern medicine is the provision of abortions. Unsurprisingly, this has sparked much debate over the years, and I have reflected regularly on the issue.

Howard urges limits of 'too easy' abortions

In what may be a first for this site, I'm actually agreeing with Tony Blair. Don't worry, I'm not going to be making a habit of it, but if abortion is to become an election issue, then I'll have to support him on it.

Michael Howard's position:

> I think that what we have now is tantamount to abortion on demand. I believe abortion should be available to everyone, but the law should be changed. In the past I voted for a restriction to 22 weeks, and I would be prepared to go down to 20.

I don't see what good would be done by reducing the age at which abortion can take place, and I see no scientific evidence for doing so. Mr Howard is responding to the pro-life propaganda pictures of foetuses that look like people. Jelly babies also look a bit like people, but I have no ethical dilemmas when it comes to munching my way through a packet.

Charles Kennedy:

> I don't know what I would do now

That's not what one would call a well argued thought out position on the issue. And if *he* doesn't know his position, how am *I* supposed to know it? And, indeed, if I don't know his position on key election issues, how am I supposed to vote for him? Come on Charlie, you can do better than this…

Tony Blair:

> However much I might dislike the idea of abortion, you should not criminalise a woman who, in very difficult circumstances, makes that choice. Obviously there is a time beyond which you can't have an abortion, and we have no plans to change that, although the debate will continue.

I know that this will come as a surprise, but - finally - I agree with Mr Blair on this. I'd perhaps go slightly further than him, because he's left himself open to attack over women who aren't in 'very difficult circumstances' but still obtain abortions, but he's in a pretty solid position. For the first time in this not-quite-an-election-campaign, I can say: Well done, Mr Blair!

/ Posted 13th March 2005

BMA votes against lowering abortion limit

My union has helpfully agreed with my position on the lowering of the 24 week limit on abortions. Whilst I'm sure this will enrage the *Daily Mail*, it certainly cheered me up because, as far as I can see, there is no logical scientific reason for lowering the abortion limit.

The only scientific reason for doing so is because increasingly premature babies are surviving with medical assistance. But whilst that's a reasonable scientific point, the logic isn't present. Increasingly premature babies are going to continue to survive as medical technology improves, until eventually abortions will be impossible - or, more controversially - they will only be available to those who discover their pregnancy suitably early, thus probably disenfranchising those who are not expecting to become pregnant (and may therefore feel that they are in desperate need of an abortion). Very few of the campaigners supporting the idea of lowering the limit would support either of the above situations - and yet that is effectively what they are voting for.

The other popularly posited opinion is that now we have 3D scans, which allow us to see the foetus in greater detail than ever, we shouldn't allow abortions at this stage of pregnancy. This is a foolish notion. Doctors have for many years seen the real foetus following abortion, and the foetus has always been at the same stage of development, even if it's previously required a medical degree to interpret the images. Just because something can now be interpreted by the masses doesn't change the nature of what is actually done.

Therefore, I agree with my BMA colleagues in their decision not to support the lowering of the abortion limit from 24 weeks to 20 weeks. And I will continue to hold that position, until I hear a reasoned logical and scientific reason to change it.

/ Posted 30th June 2005

Abortion rates hit all-time high

It seems natural to return to a subject I've often posted about for my 700th post, and an article published today by *The Guardian* allows me to do just that:

> The number of legal abortions carried out on women living in England and Wales last year was the highest ever, up more than 3,800 on 2003.

I think I've made my abortion views fairly clear over past posts - abortion isn't something I particularly like, but nor is it something I feel should be criminalised, as this penalises only the most desperate.

What's shocked me in this case, though, is not the figures themselves, but the Department of Health's response:

> The DoH said: "It is disappointing that the overall level of abortions has increased this year."

What possible authority does the Department of Health think it has to pontificate about the decisions desperate people take, and to call them 'disappointing'? The health service should be about providing unconditional help to the needy, not judging them. Their comments naturally imply that abortions are a 'bad thing', without recognising that they are often medically necessary, and that it is really the parents' decision as to what is a 'bad thing' for them.

The Department of Health would never dream of saying that it's 'disappointing' that suicide levels have increased, or that it's 'disappointing' that poor diets mean diabetes is on the increase. Why is it any different for a parent who feels so desperate that they have to go through the appalling procedure of abortion, often meaning (in the case of later abortions within the legal period) that they have to go through a full birthing process, producing a stillborn foetus? Until the righteous right realise that getting an abortion is rarely as easy as having a tooth removed, then they can't even begin to understand the mental anguish it confers upon the parent.

Could there be any greater example of the 'nanny state' than saying that the result of one of the hardest decisions a person has had to take in their whole life is 'disappointing'? I think not: It is truly abhorrent that figures relating to the most vulnerable are being given a populist spin to appease *Daily Mail* readers and secure political gains.

/ Posed 30th July 2005

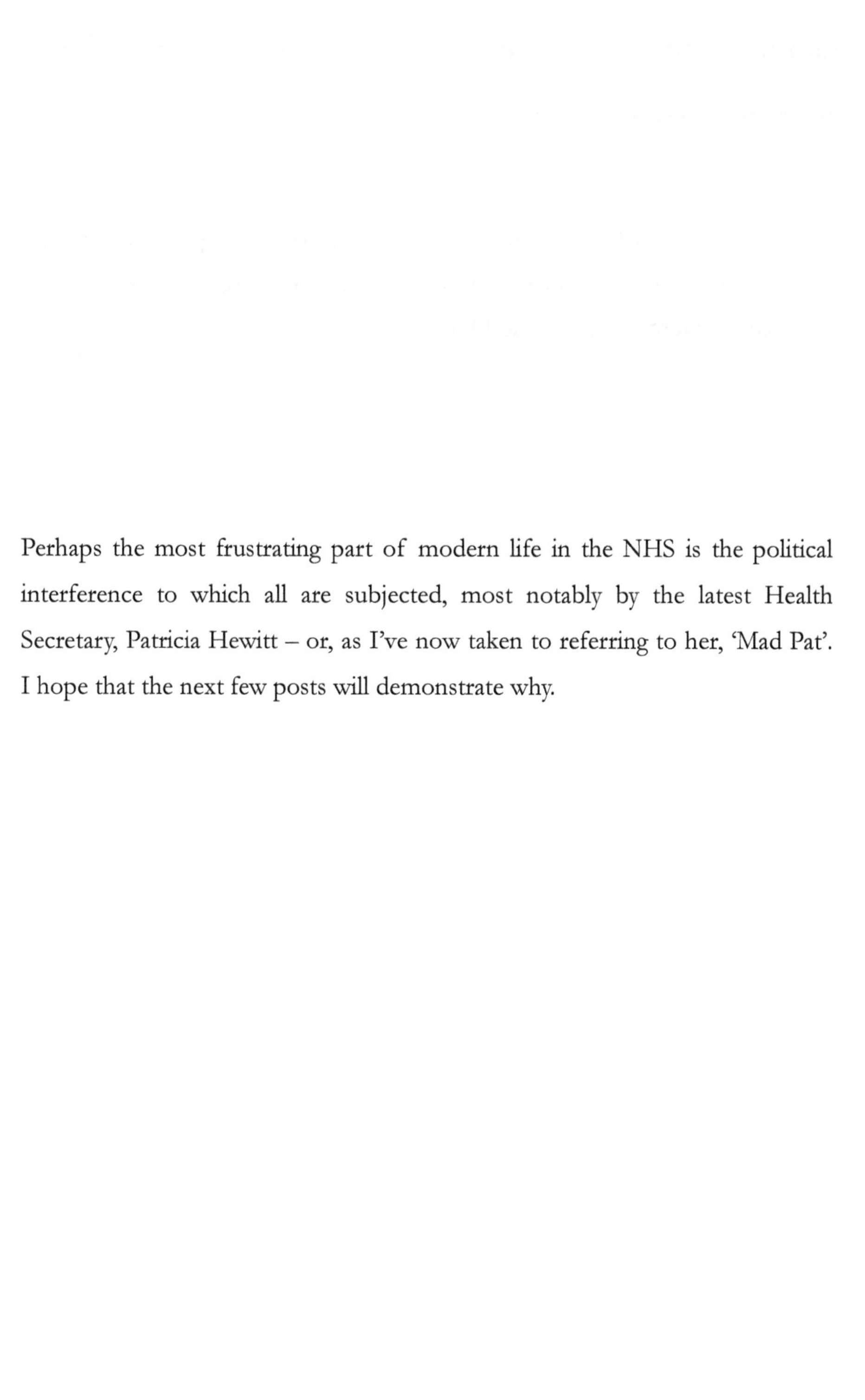

Perhaps the most frustrating part of modern life in the NHS is the political interference to which all are subjected, most notably by the latest Health Secretary, Patricia Hewitt – or, as I've now taken to referring to her, 'Mad Pat'. I hope that the next few posts will demonstrate why.

Labour wants GPs to treat diabetes, arthritis, and asthma

According to today's *Guardian*:

> GPs will provide a wider range of services, taking in areas which were once the preserve of traditional hospital care under government plans unveiled today.

This seems like an excellent idea, given how many GPs we have sitting around doing nothing. When I phone my GP, he practically begs me to come down because he's bored out of his brain.

But seriously, how does the Health Secretary, John 'Attack Dog' Reid, really expect to be able to squeeze even more people into the GP queue, especially when he's busy encouraging GPs to abolish their appointment systems? People with chronic diseases inevitably need regular care, which lends itself to an appointment system, not the 'phone-up-on-the-day' system that Reid is advocating for GP Practices in order to meet his waiting list targets.

At the same time as announcing a whole raft of new responsibilities for GPs to take on, he's also announcing

> I want to free up our GPs to be all they can be in providing services of a wider range, more conveniently, to patients.

And don't forget today's other NHS story:

> The NHS is failing to provide adequate family doctor services for patients needing emergency care outside of normal office hours, it emerged today.

So, to summarise, we don't have enough GPs to go around. Labour's way of fixing this is to force a whole new set of responsibilities and patients onto GPs, hence freeing them up to provide better services more conveniently to patients.

And Labour says the Conservatives' plans don't add up.

/ *Posted 29th March 2005*

Blair admits he doesn't know what he's doing

Blair has admitted that he doesn't know the effect he's GP waiting time targets have on patient care. He didn't realise that it was impossible to make appointments in advance. He's clearly not a dedicated fan of this site, then, because it's an issue I identified months ago.

But, more importantly, how can we re-elect a leader that introduces silly targets, and then ignores - or, more accurately, doesn't even make an effort to find out about - the problems these targets create?

And the particularly hilarious thing is that even after having the situation explained by members of the public John Reid, still doesn't get it:

> John Reid, the health secretary, acknowledged that there were problems but stressed that the target had produced much quicker access for many patients. A few years ago, many patients had to wait a week to 10 days to see a GP, he said, while on the latest figures, 97 per cent are seen within two days.

The reason 97 per cent are seen within two days is because you're only allowed to make an appointment within two days. It isn't an improvement. That's the problem. Patient satisfaction has *fallen.*

/ Posted 30th April 2005

Hewitt wants to ditch 'unpopular' NHS services

This mildly absurd plan, published in today's *Guardian*, made me smile this evening:

> The health secretary, Patricia Hewitt, today signaled that NHS hospitals face the possibility of closure if they fail to attract sufficient numbers of patients.
>
> Speaking at the International Convention Centre in Birmingham in her first public address as the newly appointed health secretary, Ms Hewitt echoed her predecessor, John Reid, by saying it was possible that some services could close if patients deserted them.

So any departments that don't attract a critical number of patients will be closed? Surely this means that there will no longer be treatment available on the NHS for anything rare…

> "Hi doc, I think I was bitten by a deadly spider on my holidays, and now I've turned a peculiar colour and my heart is failing"
>
> "Sorry, can't help, not enough people have that problem"

And will we see doctors inflicting obscure injuries, in order that their speciality be saved?

Another ill-thought out plan…

> Fears around NHS service closures circle around the introduction of a new NHS funding system, Payment by Results, whose roll out coincides with the expansion of patient choice. Under the new

> financial arrangements, money follows patients more directly, with treatments paid to hospitals - whether in the NHS or the private sector - according to a set of national tariffs (standard price).
>
> This means that if far fewer patients choose a certain hospital, an NHS trust could face a dramatic loss of funds, leading to possible closure.

So a minor surgery clinic, specialising in in-growing toenails which presumably get only a small tariff will no longer have the funding to hire a receptionist and have the heating on in the winter, because it doesn't attract the huge money that goes to the big transplant centre down the road.

Whilst clearly batty, Patricia Hewitt does fit rather more comfortably in the role of Health Secretary than John Reid. At least now you can have a concerned looking softly spoken minister saying 'I'm terribly sorry, we can't do that for you' instead of a rather less comforting man yelling 'No, I won't fix you, and there was no need to ask me in that tone of voice.'

All we need now is an appropriate and competent minister. When's the next election?

/ Posted 13th May 2005

'Mad' Patricia Hewitt strikes again

Ms Hewitt's spell of virtual insanity continues, with her now announcing that she wants to make those who spread MRSA criminals:

> Private cleaning contractors, managers and even visitors could face criminal liability for spreading the hospital superbug MRSA in the NHS.

What does Ms Hewitt hope to achieve by making spreading MRSA a crime? To do so would mean that doctors would have to take every possible step to avoid litigation - is she seriously suggesting that all doctors should have a full surgical scrub before seeing every patient? That would more than triple the length of the average consultation, so I hope she's got some money squirreled away for lots of extra doctors. And what about the emergency situation? Are we all to completely scrub up before performing emergency procedures? A few more deaths might well be occurring if that's expected.

MRSA will only be brought under control with sensible steps to educate medical staff and the public about prevention, and the necessary funding to keep hygiene standards up. If the funding had been available to put alcohol gel next to every bed five or six years ago - instead of only just getting round to it - then MRSA wouldn't be such a big a problem now. Threatening people with litigation is simply absurd, and deeply unhelpful. And if she's going to start slapping fines on cleaning companies, standards are unlikely to improve much but costs will sky-rocket. So I hope there's lots of money available for the government to pay its own fines, too.

/ Posted 16th May 2005

Mad Pat redefines 'stabilising'

The NHS is now in £521,000,000 debt. That's quite a lot. More than twice as much as this time last year, in fact.

When responding to the last set of figures last December, Patricia Hewitt, our esteemed Health Secretary, announced that she would have the debt down to £250,000,000 by April. It's now June, and she's nowhere near - in fact, she's heading in the wrong direction altogether, despite firing 12,000 people, cancelling countless operations, and reducing the quality of patient care. Yet today in Mad Pat's world…

> The NHS is now stabilising this financial problem while counting to improve services for patients.

Doubling of debt equals 'stabilising this financial problem'. This new definition is very handy. Blood pressure doubled in 12 months? Don't bother treating it, it's stable! Tumour size doubled? Don't worry about that cancelled op, your tumour's stable! Think of the savings that can be made!

Doctors can see what's wrong here. The BMA Consultants Committee said

> Yes, bad management is a problem in some places, but the biggest cause is the interference from government. Something is going badly wrong and it is demoralising for staff.

We know the nurses are against her following the extraordinary action at their conference. Doctors are quite clearly against her. And, hey-ho, the

Confederation of the managers Mad Pat was so criticised for introducing in the first place is even against her:

> It is all too easy to blame individual managers, but the financial problems often relate to systemic issues.

And, surprise surprise, the Opposition knows what's wrong:

> Policy is failing.

So who's backing Mad Pat? Well, apparently, Mr Blair. Despite her coming out with meaningless misjudged announcement after meaningless misjudged announcement, even after missing her own targets by miles, there's still no suggestion that she might be unfit for the position.

Nobody in the NHS likes her, she polls badly, and she doesn't meet targets. Why on Earth is she still in office?

/ Posted 7th June 2006

Hospital to treat pets to reduce debts?

From the Press Association:

> A cash-strapped hospital could open its doors to dogs and cats in a bid to raise extra funds, it has emerged.
>
> Ipswich Hospital is proposing to use its state-of-the-art radiotherapy equipment, which lies dormant at weekends, to treat family pets with cancer at special Saturday morning clinics.

It's like something from *The Thick of It.* When the NHS is so cash-strapped that hospitals are thinking of treating animals, things aren't going well. Why do I suspect the hand of Mad Pat in this? Just to remind you, other proposals she's come up with include closing unpopular hospital departments, making those who spread MRSA face criminal charges, announcing that the doubling of NHS debt means the financial crisis is 'stabilising', and, perhaps most famously, announcing that this year was the NHS's 'best year ever'. Compared to those gaffes, suggesting that NHS hospitals start treating pets seems relatively sane.

How is this woman still in her job?

/ Posted 29th October 2006

Hewitt: NHS has too many doctors and nurses

Everybody's favourite giant-flower wearing government jester, Heath Secretary 'Mad' Patricia Hewitt, has decreed that

> some parts of the NHS in England have taken on too many doctors and nurses

That seems a bit of a sweeping statement to me. I think it's important she's more specific - exactly which hospitals have too many doctors and nurses? Presumably not the one in Wales, which has had to close its minor injuries unit due to a lack of staff. Presumably not Scotland, where current government estimates say there will soon be 500 too few GPs - a number the BMA believes to be much higher. And presumably not England, where ambulances have been turned away from understaffed A&Es.

But they're out there somewhere. And it's important we find them. After all, we can't go spending all the NHS money on silly extravagances like doctors and nurses when there's marketing to be paid for.

So where are these wasteful hospitals? Fellow blogger Dr Crippen is looking for them. I want to know where they are. And I'm sure the electorate surrounding the identified hospitals will be interested.

So come on, Pat, tell us: Which hospitals have too many healthcare staff?

/ Posted 22nd November 2006

MTAS: Breaks spirits, breaks doctors, breaks the law

I've lost count of the number of times I've said Mad Pat should resign. I'm starting to get a reputation. But she really is not fit for purpose. After presiding over a catalogue of failures, she's still in post.

She thinks services for rare diseases should be scrapped, doctors and nurses who don't wash their hands should go to prison, hospitals should treat animals alongside humans, that NHS debt doubling is a good thing, that the NHS has too many doctors and nurses, and that dirty sheets are the way forward. She's presided over an absolutely catastrophic failure in reform of medical training, and yet still thinks the NHS has just enjoyed its best year ever. She's even cut the most vital of services because it's not a political priority.

And now, it's revealed that not only was MTAS a failure in selecting the right people for the right jobs, it was also a total security shambles.

Thousands of medical students' and junior doctors' personal details - including mobile phone numbers, addresses, and even criminal records - were posted, unprotected, on the internet, for anyone to access. They're even available on Google.

As if that wasn't enough, highly sensitive personal data which was supposed to be stored *anonymously* and *separately from personal data* - things like sexuality and religion - have been posted on the internet alongside the applicants' names.

When this was first reported to the NHS's IT commission, they said 'Ah, there's not much we can do about that'. *That's* when the doctors went to the media. Then Lord Hunt comes along and claims that these were posted by some malicious individual. *That was not true.* Then it was claimed that the details had only been visible on the web for a few hours. *That was also not true.* The system was so badly designed that this data was simply being stored online, without even simple password protection, and had been available to anyone with an internet connection and a titter of wit for *at least three days*, and almost certainly much, much longer.

But just in case that's not terrible enough, it has emerged today that not only could such information be downloaded and seen by anyone with an internet connection, but it could also be edited. By anyone. Yep, anyone could get into any applicants online application and edit it to their heart's content without so much as a password.

This is not only incredibly shoddy security, it's also *illegal.* It's quite clearly against the Data Protection Act, and legal experts are predicting that if any junior doctor decides to sue the government over this, then they've got a pretty decent chance of winning the case.

But heck, that's not enough for this failure of a government.

The system which is currently being tested to hold patient records has managed to spew out the personal details of many consultants, including their home addresses and phone numbers. This is the apparently super-secure system that is virtually impossible to hack, spewing out personal details onto the internet in a completely unprotected fashion.

Patricia Hewitt has presided over the introduction of a system which has destroyed confidence, made lives hell for junior doctors, and now broken the law. She's been an unmitigated failure of a Health Secretary, and has done damage to the NHS that will take years to put right.

I don't think I can ask her to resign again. The fact that she's been through all this and not even considered tendering her resignation tells us everything we need to know about her, and everything we need to know about New Labour, and everything we need to know about political integrity. There's none left.

/ Posted 26th April 2007

MTAS: Unbelievably, it gets worse

I thought we'd hit rock bottom yesterday. Once you've openly and illegally posted intimate details about applicants on the internet, I didn't think there was anywhere else to go. I was wrong.

The failed system has been shut down. But now, thanks to an utterly contemptible lack of contingency planning, doctors don't know if they've got interviews *next week*, or even where and when the interviews will be held.

MTAS was supposed to make NHS job applications more like the private sector. Do companies really try and attract people to work for them for the next thirty-five years by ignoring their past work-related experience, posting their intimate personal details all over the internet, and then not telling them when and where their interviews are? Is that how Mad Pat was appointed?

It's also emerged that after a failure of the security of MTAS's predecessor MDAP, the BMA was promised by the government that the new system would be super-secure. Now we know that not even a password was needed to access thousands of people's personal details. And I guess we also know the value of a government 'promise'.

We no longer have anywhere near enough NHS dentists thanks to this government's policies. Soon, we won't have any doctors either.

/ Posted 27th April 2007

MTAS: Doctors want Hewitt to go

There's a danger of this turning into the MTAS blog at the moment, but I can't hide my incredulity at the complete and utter failure MTAS has been.

Now it emerges that Patricia Hewitt was told about the problems with MTAS security by the British Orthopaedics Trainees Association *a month ago*, yet chose to do absolutely nothing about it. She *knew* that intimate details about doctors' personal lives could be viewed by others, and even modified by them, and yet chose to take *no action*. If that doesn't make her personally liable for prosecution under the Data Protection Act, I'm not sure what would.

Lord Hunt has confirmed today that the MTAS system is down, and he's no idea when it will be back up. Until then, doctors will be missing interviews, because there is no mechanism in place to communicate the times and dates of these interviews to them. And he refuses to guarantee that the process of matching doctors to jobs will be completed by the August deadline. What he plans to do if it's not is a mystery: Leave doctors without jobs and hospitals without doctors?

Patricia Hewitt has agreed to appear on *Channel 4 News* next week. Other than resigning live on air, I'm not sure what she can say or do to make up for this absolute shambles. Junior doctors have today voted for her to go, and I don't know if she can survive the pressure long enough to go when Blair goes, as she inevitably will. It's just a shame that won't fix the problem.

/ Posted 28th April 2007

Crime and Punishment

Like healthcare, one of the biggest responsibilities of any government is the introduction and policing of new law. Some governments do this extremely effectively. In my opinion, this Labour Government has not. Here is some of my writing on everyday crimes – and the government's ways of tackling them – over the life of sjhoward.co.uk.

Capital punishment

Following the killing of PC Beshenivsky, several people who should know better have been calling for the reintroduction of the death penalty for those who kill police officers. This is a pretty silly proposal, as anyone with a handful of brain cells can recognise.

First and foremost, why is the death of a police officer any more terrible than the death of someone with a different job? Why is it more terrible than the killing of a child? Heck, why is it more terrible to kill a *single* police officer than it is to kill a tower block full of civvies? Especially when you consider that police officers are actively remunerated for the risk that they may be harmed on duty?

Secondly, people who kill police, by definition, do not expect to be caught. They're killing the police either in a moment of clouded judgement or because they think they're going to get away. No criminal is going to stand there and say 'Fair cop, guv, slap the ol' han'cuffs on then' just because killing a police officer carries the death penalty, because they're not considering the penalty at the time of the crime.

Thirdly, if we go about killing people based on a single decision taken in a split second, set against the background of their whole life, why are we any better than the criminals?

This proposal serves no serious purpose other than to allow some barbaric form of satisfaction for the bereaved. And, frankly, I thought humanity was better than that.

/ Posted 24th November 2005

Licensing Hours

I'm not sure where I stand on the issue of increasing licensing hours.

On the good side, there's clearly a big need to change this country's attitude to drink, and a change of attitude is most easily brought about by a change in society. As somebody who doesn't go out to get drunk, I can't profess to understand why people do this, but I'm sure that people who do it are aware of the probable consequences, and are not going to stop drinking with more forcefully imparted knowledge of these. A cultural change is needed. If that cultural change can be brought about by changing licensing hours, then so be it. This change would also end the problem of all of the pubs closing at 11pm, and the streets being unbearably roudy at this particular time. And it's simply scaremongering to say that pubs will be open twenty-four hours, since very few places will be able to afford the staff to serve the three local drunks at four in the morning.

On the less-good side, there's yet to be an extensive trial of these changes, so who can really say whether or not this will change attitudes to drink. If the extension of licensing hours doesn't result in the desired change in attitudes, then we're left with a terrible situation where people will sit and drink themselves silly for much of the night. And it could replace one big period of disturbance with a continuous trickle throughout the night, which would consequently be more difficult to avoid and affect more people.

So I think that we need to have a large-scale trial before we decide whether to go ahead with this idea. I've heard the Government pointing to our European neighbours of examples where long licensing hours are not a problem, which does nothing but introduce a chicken-and-egg argument about attitudes to drink and the relevant licensing regulations.

> With public concern rising, the Conservatives are now suggesting the liberalisation of hours should be delayed until binge drinking is curbed.

I'll respect this position when the Tories get round to explaining how they intend to tackle the binge drinking problem. The shameful position they have adopted on this is opportunism at its most infuriating. It's criticising the Government for the binge drinking problem, and criticising it for trying radical ways to fix it. This isn't a sensible place to be in an election year, because it makes the Tories appear to lack credibility. Given the current opinion polls (and common sense), this is something they should probably try to avoid weeks before an election.

> Medical opinion argues there will be no lessening of alcohol problems until the cost of drink returns to the relative prices of the 1970s. This would imply doubling the price of a £4 bottle of wine and pushing up beer to £5 a pint.

I'm not sure whose medical opinion this is, but it certainly isn't mine. Doubling the price of alcohol will simply replace one problem with another: Alcoholics, who are found in a higher proportion of poor-income families, will be spending even more money to get their fix and driving themselves even further into the depths of poverty. Increased prices may help to stem the tide of binge drinkers in middle England, but they shouldn't be helped at the expense of those worse off in society. Increasing prices would bring about a cultural change, but not the one we're looking for.

If I was given the task of reducing the level of binge drinking in society, I know where I'd start - by asking the people who do it why they do it. If only the

Government would take this approach, then maybe they could treat the root cause of the problem rather than the symptoms.

That's my medical opinion.

/ Posted 23rd January 2005

Tagging non-paying parents

I read today that the Government is considering electronically tagging parents who fail to pay child support (rather unfortunately phrased by *BBC News* as 'those dads who are not paying for their kids', but let's not get into that). A simple question: Why?

The idea is to restrict the movements of people who don't pay up. How on Earth will that help? Dad doesn't have any money to give mum, mum doesn't have any money, the child grows up in poverty. What does tagging achieve? Dad doesn't have any money to give mum, dad's movements are restricted and employability reduced so he has less chance to make some money, mum doesn't have any money, the child grows up in poverty.

Yes, there are some parents who refuse to pay child support on principle. But they're already able to be sentenced to six weeks in prison. Surely tagging is a lesser threat, and hence less likely to make people comply? Of course, the politicians seem to be suggesting that it's 'easier' to tag someone than to send them to prison. Certainly for the CSA itself, it should make no difference, as a prosecution in a Court of Law is presumably needed for either, and given that tagging is supposed to replicate the loss of freedom in prison, surely a similar burden of proof is needed.

The CSA has never really worked properly in its entire history. It currently costs £1 in administration for every £1.85 recovered, and that doesn't include the cost of the prosecutions handled by the judiciary, which also comes from taxpayer's pockets. All in all, it probably costs more to recover the money than it would to just hand it out. Even Mr Blair, who rarely dares admit such a thing, says it doesn't do it's job properly (though why it's taken him eight years to find that out is something of a mystery). Can we not just put it out of its misery?

Well, under a Labour government, probably not until they've come up with something even more bureaucratic to replace it. Why not do the simple thing of handing the job over to the Inland Revenue and taking the money out of people's pay packet directly? Then there's no chasing to be done, and far less administration, and far less chance of people failing to pay. But then, that's probably too simple a solution.

/ Posted 3rd January 2006

Reasons for teenage knife crime

In a perverse way, the ongoing coverage of teenage knife crime amuses me. Tabloids will insist that all teenagers are delinquents, and yet come August, they all have 25 A-Levels as a result of dumbing down. In reality, only a minority of teenagers sit A-Levels (let alone pass them), and far fewer still are 'bad kids' (no matter how they might look).

And let me bust one more myth. We are not in the middle of a knife-crime explosion. Knife crime has been at reasonably consistent levels over the last ten years. It's reasonable to hypothesise that the teenagers of 1996 were involved in just as many knife crimes as the teenagers of 2006. There have been around five fatal stabbings per week for the last ten years. There has been no dramatic increase. But suddenly, every one of those five has become headline news. It's being noticed more, but it isn't happening more. Sorry to burst the dead-tree media bubble.

But that doesn't answer the crucial question: Why is there teenage knife crime on our streets?

It's nothing to do with a lack of activities for teenagers. If you apply that theory to any other section of society, its flaws are clear. Did Ian Huntley commit the Soham Murders because he didn't have a social worker to take him bowling every week? Did Harold Shipman bump off old people because he didn't have a club of like-minded individuals to socialise with in a controlled setting? Was Hitler a community volunteering project away from sticking with painting and decorating? I think not.

And it's nothing to do with the prevalence of knives on the streets, either. Sixty years ago, knives were much more common amongst teenagers, and teenagers were also much more adept with the use of guns thanks to National Service. Weapons don't kill people: People kill people.

Also sixty years ago, there was a very clear, defined enemy. The Germans. Teenagers would probably have had little hesitation in taking out their frustration on any Germans they happened upon, but fortunately that didn't happen very often. They were rebels with a very defined cause, and a cause which society supported and viewed as 'healthy'.

So what's the 'cause' today? Who are our enemies?

In the absence of a clear enemy, society as a whole has started to attack within its own group. Football rivalries become as embittered as those between warring nations, and so violence ensues. Rivalries between middle-class parents to get their children into the schools at the top of artificial league-tables get out of hand. Minor road incidents turn into violent road rage. And rivalries between gangs of friends escalate to stabbings. It's not rocket science.

As a nation, we have nothing to unite against and fight. Yet we have a human need for rivalry and fighting, so in the absence of a defined enemy, we fight each other. It's happening throughout all age groups and in many walks of life, but because the media has an obsession with demonising the youth, it's this that gets highlighted.

This is not the end of society as we know it. We do not have a generation of evil teenagers. It's a natural development, which will probably subside as the nation becomes united again behind some visionary cause.

So please, just for me, can we stop harassing these poor teenagers? Life's tough enough for them without criminalising them with silly ASBOs, slapping discriminatory policies all over them, and constantly criticising them.

Fix the behaviour of your own generation before criticising theirs.

/ Posted 9th April 2007

Legislation pretends to ban ageism

Today is one of those wonderful days where an unfortunate confluence of events means that we can see through the government's spin and political correctness, and gawp at the real decisions being taken in Whitehall.

Today, new legislation comes into force, spun as 'banning ageism'. Reporting on these new rules, *BBC News* says:

> They make it unlawful to discriminate against workers under the age of 65 on the grounds of age.
>
> The rules will impact on recruitment, training, promotion, redundancy, retirement, pay and pension provision.

Ministers have been popping up here, there, and everywhere over the last week emphasising that not only does this rule out discrimination against older people, it also protects the young from being discriminated against in favour of the old. Which is all fine and dandy, but sadly untrue.

Giving the lie to the spin is another new piece of legislation coming into force today: An increase in the minimum wage. Despite ageism now being illegal, this continues to have three tiers. 16 and 17 year olds receive a minimum of £3.30 per hour, 18 to 21 year olds receive a minimum £4.85, whilst over 21s get £5.35.

Ageism is, apparently, outlawed, but if I were to go and get a proper job today, I could be paid 50p an hour less than somebody less than six-months my senior. From where I'm standing, that smells a lot like ageism.

So it's fairly clear that the government's actual target here is the older generation. By preventing employers from retiring people at sixty based on age alone, perhaps the government think that this will become the norm, before they force it to be so by raising the official retirement age. But it's a bit of a stretch even for New Labour to pretend to be discouraging ageism on the same day as retaining an increasing a three-tier minimum wage.

But thank you, Tony, for showing us how to ban ageism whilst simultaneously actively promoting it. I don't think anyone else could.

/ Posted 1st October 2006

Where not to put your foot down

I still don't get why people are so annoyed about prosecution of speeding motorists. This is, effectively, a crackdown on crime. Surely we should be hailing the capture of more criminals as a success - even if they are motorists.

Speed cameras may not be the best way of catching people, but if they work then what's wrong with that? They're not invading privacy, they're not affecting the lives of innocent people, they're just catching those people who will insist on *breaking the law.*

Just because people disagree with a law does not give them the right to ignore it. Perhaps I happen to think that murder and rape are unjustly made illegal - does this give me a right to do either of these as much as I like? I certainly hope not.

As I've said over and over, if people don't like speed cameras, then stop speeding so that there are no fines to fund them. They'll soon disappear.

/ Posted 13th February 2005

ID cards and the constitution

A trail starts on Monday of the proposed ID cards…but what do you think of them? I'm personally against them really, since I don't think they will be of benefit. The arguments put forward for them are, generally…

Prevent illegal immigration

I can't see how this can be the case. Why will an illegal immigrant find it any more difficult to 'disappear'? They don't have any identification documents at the moment, so why will not having a card hinder them? Unless, of course, we're going to be forced to produce them at request, which we're told is not the case, and is a very dangerous route to take.

Prevent illegal working

Most employers who have illegal workers know that the workers are illegal. Besides which, we all have National Insurance numbers that can (and should) do this anyway.

Aid anti-terrorism measures

If I'm going to fly a jumbo jet into a towerblock, why will a plastic card stop me? The Spanish have identity cards, and they've suffered one of the worst terrorist attacks of modern times.

Tackle identity theft

This depends very much on how they are used, and if they are used as I suspect, as a single identity document in themselves, then stealing this card immediately opens you to identity theft. Biometric data is only useful for those who have readers, and photographs don't prevent someone passing themselves off as someone else, as we see with stolen Passports every day.

Reduce benefit fraud and abuse of public services

We have a number of systems already in place to ensure that public services are only used by those entitled. If these were properly enforced, which would be a much cheaper option, then there would be no need for any new system (eg you are supposed to take your NHS Card each time you go to the doctors….Do you?)

Enhance sense of community

Tell me this is a joke. If I was racist, I would still be racist whether or not the other person had a card.

I do understand that they would be a handy form of ID, but that's an argument against them. When you have to provide two forms of photo ID, it's hard to find them, you have to go searching to dig out your passport and driving licence (or similar). If you have this card on you all the time, and your driving licence, then there's two forms of photo ID that are stolen right off the bat if your bag is stolen.

The whole point of this ID process is that it's difficult for the real person, and so almost impossible for a fraudster.

So why ask us all to pay £35 for a card that is pointless?

/ Posted 25th April 2004

ID cards bill given second reading

I'm disappointed, but not surprised, to see this on the *BBC News* homepage:

> Government wins key Commons vote on ID Cards Bill by majority of 31. More soon.

With Labour's majority severely reduced, I was hoping that pointless legislation would no longer get through the House of Commons. Yet, even after watching the debate for most of the afternoon, I still see no reason for ID cards to be introduced. Maybe I'm just stupid.

One of the main arguments for ID cards in recent days, and the one apparently favoured by Mr Blair, has been that biometric passports are being introduced, and we might as well have ID cards at the same time. To me, this makes no sense. Only people who apply for the new passports will get ID cards, so why not use their passports as ID?

Charles Clarke has now conceded that ID cards won't really help in the fight against crime, but does claim that they'll help against serious and organised crime - the example he chose to cite on the *Today* programme was drug smuggling. Why would anyone smuggling drugs do so with a fake ID? It would just be one further possible trigger for suspicion. Somebody trying to smuggle drugs into the country would surely do so in a way as to appear as inconspicuous as possible. If they're currently trying to do that using forged passports, then I suggest their logic is slightly twisted.

As for terrorism: The people who commit terrorist offences rarely use fake ID. Again, using fake ID only increases the chance of getting caught. The key to successfully committing a terrorist offence is surely to use people who would not raise any suspicion in their day-to-day lives, but are under the control of the lead fundamentalists. Not to try and get through security checks with fake ID.

And finally, the argument put forward that this should serve as a single form of unquestionable ID is dangerous. The ID cards are to carry three pieces of biometric data, since using only one doesn't provide suitable efficacy. Now Charles Clarke is making a big deal of the fact that this will mean you'll no longer have to collect lots of documents together to open a bank account, get a library card, or get a copy of your criminal record in a CRB check. Unless he's planning on equipping every bank, library, and CRB representative (which include thousands of members of councils, universities, churches, and youth groups) with an iris scanner, facial recognition software, and fingerprinting devices, then these people will not be able to check the biometric data, and so these cards end up being no more secure in day-to-day use than normal photographic ID. So to then announce that this will serve as a sole form of ID makes it much easier to commit identity theft offences, as only one document will need to be forged.

So as far as I can see, our elected representatives have voted to divulge far more about our lives than ever before to governmental departments, and allow them to store this data on computers that will probably not be as secure as they should be, and that will probably cost more than the government says, for no tangible benefit. And the majority wasn't even *that* narrow. Good one, guys.

/ Posted 28th June 2005

Third of DVLA car records wrong

According to *BBC News* today, a third of all car record held by the DVLA are wrong.

Cars would seem a very simple set of items on which to keep a database since, other than ownership details, very little changes from the day they are created to the day they land on the scrap heap. But this report implies that even the registration numbers, which (for the majority of vehicles) do not change over the lifetime of the car are wrong in many cases.

If the Government can't even manage to keep a correct database of cars, how on Earth am I expected to believe that it can keep an accurate database of people, which will inevitably have many more variables which change more frequently?

Earlier this month, I wrote to the local council to inform them that me and my housemate were exempt from Council Tax, enclosing the relevant exemption certificates. They then wrote back, requesting my Council Tax. They had applied the certificate, which had my name, date of birth, and address on it, to the wrong account, and so had someone incorrectly registered as exempt, and me incorrectly registered as owing money. Again, this seems a relatively simple process of updating the records of the person whose details are sat in front of you, and yet the council were unable to do this.

If the Government has a proven track record of failures like these, why does anyone trust them to keep an accurate database of information as the back-end to an ID cards system? And is it not worrying that mistakes could easily be made in an apparently 'infallible' system, which could lead to terrible consequences for those whose details are wrong?

As I've said before, ID cards are unnecessary and I would've voted against them. But these recent developments just reminded me how dangerously fallible the system could be.

/ Posted 28th January 2005

Feeling protected?

SOCA (Serious Organised Crime Agency) has launched today. No doubt they'll lock up all the naughty criminals, probably without trial. In fact, they might just start detaining people at birth, or killing everyone with a padded jacket. After all, from a flashy (expensive) looking press-room, Mr Blair announced they're going to make life 'hell' for 'Mr Bigs'. The easiest, most-efficient way to do this is to shoot or detain everyone who looks a little bit dodgy. So that's probably what'll happen.

And they have a fantastically New Labour target: 'To reduce harm'. Prove they've succeeded or failed at that!

But what about all the criminals who aren't serious? What about those who are just killing people for a bit of a laugh? They're going to thrive! Extreme custard-pie throwings a-go-go! I think the government have missed a trick… and made an appropriate acronym: After all, crime is all a bit of a political sport to Mr Blair.

/ Posted 3rd April 2006

The Home Office's latest abject failure

It's at times like this when I begin to wonder why we bother with the Home Office.

After a series of Home Office blunders and Home Secretary resignations, the incoming John Reid said the Home Office was 'not fit for purpose'. He gives himself 100 days to fix the problem, and proudly announces 'job done'. Then, as if by magic, yet another abject failure on the part of the Home Office is revealed.

The hugely complicated bureaucratic beast that is the outsourced Criminal Records Bureau is shown once again to be less than perfect: If anyone had committed a crime abroad then it would not show up on their criminal record, since no-one knew they'd committed it, police included, as the information sent by foreign officials had laid undiscovered in a file somewhere in Whitehall.

Ministers deny all knowledge, then it emerges that they were sent a letter *last year* about the problem. Presumably it was filed in the same place as the criminal records. So what excuse will be given for this mess? Probably that the letter sent acknowledging receipt of the first acknowledged merely that the letter had been received, not read. Or some such bollocks.

But at the end of the day, what does it matter? Even if the junior ministers get fired, in Blair's jobs-for-all government they'll be paid off and then rehired a few months later. It's just another example of the 'pretty straight' 'whiter-than-white' Prime Minister and his incentivised dirty government.

The obvious solution is a wholesale review and redesign of the Home Office, possibly splitting it up into several smaller departments. David Cameron's suggestion of a separate Terrorism Office is faintly ridiculous as it leaves bodies such as the Police with two governmental masters with different priorities, but the department could be split into several more manageable chunks. But it never will be, because that would involve a wholesale *spending* review, and that would never do at a bloated over-funded Home Office.

It would be nice to see some true accountability for these blunders, though. But introducing a system of proper accountability is not in the interest of any MP, so that's certainly never going to happen - whatever party leaders might want us to believe.

Let's sack the lot of 'em!

/ Posted 11th January 2007

PCs should get out of cars and walk alone

Sir Keith Povey has written an article in today's *Times* about modern policing. However experienced and respected he might be, clearly has values that are completely different to mine. He's the kind of person who'd say 'If you've done nothing wrong, then why do you fear the police?' It's actually quite scary to think that people like this are in high positions in the police force.

> Sir Keith added that inventions such as DNA profiling would revolutionise policing. He forecast that Britain would have a national database based on samples compulsorily taken at birth within a decade. Police already have a growing database of convicted and suspected criminals.

This is scary stuff. There's no way I want to live in a society where my DNA is kept on file from birth. I'm not really happy with the current situation of keeping convicted criminals' DNA records on file for life (in fact, in many ways that's less satisfactory than doing it for the whole country). The consequences of such a move could be absolutely terrible.

> 'I know the civil liberties people will argue against it but it's not just an enforcement tool; it's an identification showing people are innocent as well as guilty,' he said.
>
> 'I think we are talking about something in the next ten years. I don't think it's a big step because where are the objections in a lot of areas? The benefits of DNA are so great and go well beyond law enforcement and it's not that intrusive.'

So not only does he want to keep my DNA on file, he wants to use it as evidence that I'm guilty of a crime. DNA should certainly not be used in this situation if a national database is implemented, since it is only about 99.999975% accurate (meaning that DNA found at a crime scene could match about 15 people in the country - which is also why it's a bad idea to convict known criminals in a database based solely on DNA evidence, since the DNA would only narrow the field to 15 people (the other 14 of whom are unknown in this situation), and would not pin the crime to one person.

In a national database scenario, this could get very messy - imagine finding, through a crime investigation your DNA gets you involved in, that the person you think is your father actually is not. This is a remarkably common scenario in Britain today. What greater intrusion of civil liberties than to become one of the top suspects in a murder you didn't even know about, and have your perception of your familial relationships blown apart, on the basis of flawed DNA evidence? And yet Sir Kieth thinks this isn't intrusive. I'd hate to see what he thought *was* intrusive!

> 'If you are really serious about ID cards, it's got to be compulsory, mandatory to carry it and it has to be produced on demand to a police officer.'

Thousands of bags and wallets are stolen each year. What if yours was in this situation? Not only would you, under the current plans, be unable to claim the benefits and public services to which you are entitled (What if you were hurt in the mugging, needed to see a doctor, but couldn't do so without your card?), but now Sir Keith wants to arrest *you* for not having your card. It'd be laughable if he wasn't so serious.

> Sir Keith pointed out that a few years ago closed-circuit television cameras were attacked as a threat to civil liberties, but now communities demanded them.

This is because cameras are of such poor quality that the pictures are rarely used as the sole evidence in a case. But they still manage to cut crime, because they act as a deterrent to petty criminals. And they therefore make people feel safer, which is why they are 'demanded'. If there had been some widely publicised cases of people being wrongly convicted by virtue of CCTV pictures, then I expected they wouldn't be quite so welcomed.

> Sir Keith said he started on the beat 42 years ago in Sheffield and made his first arrest catching two men stealing scrap metal.
>
> 'In those days I always patrolled alone. In fact it was a disciplinary offence if you were caught talking to the man on the next beat, whereas now everybody patrols in pairs.
>
> 'I firmly believe there is far too much double-crewing, as we call it, whether on patrol or in vehicles. When you think officers have got sprays, side-handled batons - they don't need to be in pairs most of the time,' he said.

He may feel that way, but at a time when police-public relations are at an all time low, and violent crime is on the rise, I certainly wouldn't want to walk around on my own in a police uniform. Would you?

/ Posted 3rd January 2005

Issuing guns to all police officers

Following on from an earlier post about the suggestion that capital punishment should be brought back, today I thought I'd comment on the equally silly suggestion that all police officers should carry guns.

Before I make any argument, let's look at the figures. 11 police officers have been shot and killed in the line of duty in the UK in the last twenty years. 30 civilians have been shot and killed by police officers in the line of duty in the UK in the last twelve years. That means that about one police officer is shot dead every couple of years, while the police shoot dead five civvies in the same amount of time. To the best of my researching powers, every single one of the police officers shot dead in the last twenty years have resulted in prosecution or death of the civvy with the gun. Of the thirty civvies shot and killed, not one has resulted in a police officer with a gun being prosecuted - *even in the cases where the civvies were completely innocent.*

To me, that alone suggests that arming every police officer is not a bright idea.

Figures aside, let's think about this. The suggestion is that every police officer should be given a *two-day* training course, then sent out on the street with a gun. Frankly, after a two-day training course, they'll be lucky to be able to hit a guy at six paces without some 'collateral damage'. Then there's the medical aspect - you don't need great eye-sight to be in the police. I could be in it. But I have a squint. Should I ever try and fire a gun, I'll miss the target by a mile. What are you going to do with police like me? Not arm me, so I become the obvious target in a force of armed officers? Or kick me out, despite loyal service?

People claim that the police would only use the guns in the most extreme circumstances. To be frank, I say that's bollocks. You see a guy coming at you with a knife. You're unarmed, so, with heart thumping, you try to negotiate. Worse case scenario, you fail. You've got a knife sticking out of your abdomen, because you weren't wearing your knife-proof vest. That's not a good state to be in, but you're pretty certain to survive, and get over it, returning to complete health. Yes, it would take time, but you put yourself on the front line, that was your choice.

Now consider that you're armed. Before the guy gets to you, you pull out your gun. He keeps coming towards you. Luckily, you're quite talented at shooting, avoid the rest of the people on the busy street, and shoot and kill the guy. He ain't going to recover. He's dead. No court will ever be able to decide whether he was guilty, psychiatrically impaired, in need of help, or whatever. He's dead. He'll never get a chance to tackle his problems.

I'm by no means suggesting that *all* attackers would continue to lunge. But some would, and those would die. And that can't really be too good.

All police being armed raises the stakes of the game significantly, and means that much more premeditated crime will involve guns. If the police have them, the criminals will have to match or even beat them. Gun crime soars, the streets become inevitably more dangerous. And then there's the issue of the guns falling into the wrong hands, or even new, inexperienced police officers being attacked for their guns. Not a healthy prospect.

And the final point… It completely changes the relationship between the public and the police. For example, I'm quite heartened to see the (very) occasional police officer on the beat now and again. Would I be so heartened if I knew he was carrying a gun, and capable of lethal force? I think not. And I think some in the police would let that power go to their heads, and imagine (even more-so than now) that they are an untouchable, greater class, rather than public servants policing by consent.

So, as far as I can see, there are many more arguments of greater power for keeping the police unarmed than there are for routinely arming them. So it's not something I'd support. */ Posted 25th November 2005*

Volunteer speed police recruited

From the today's *Times*:

> Hundreds of volunteers are being trained by police to trap drivers speeding on rural roads. The "village vigilante" scheme ... has quietly expanded across large swathes of the country.

I should be raging about this. I should be up in arms about the fact that the police are essentially sanctioning and aiding vigilante action. I should be pointing out that we pay police to keep law and order in this country, and they shouldn't be out recruiting the public to do that job for them. But I can't; it just seems like too much of a good idea.

Speeding is a huge problem in this country, and an area of widespread law-breaking. You'd think that this very fact would lead politicians to reconsider the law in the first place, but it hasn't. That's neither here nor there in this discussion, though, because a lot of speeding is senselessly dangerous. Therefore, to go back to a situation where people caught speeding are not issued with a fine, but instead with advice on why they shouldn't be doing it, and thus increasing drivers' education and understanding of the problem, can only be a very good thing. The fact that the police are asking volunteers to help out with this scheme so that they can concentrate on catching 'real' criminals should surely delight *Daily Mail* readers everywhere.

These volunteers have no police powers. They're simply issuing advice to motorists. It's no different to charities advising kids not to get into drugs because they can be seriously detrimental to health. So whilst I'm less than impressed with other 'community policing' measures such as CSOs, this doesn't seem such a bad idea to me. So I'd broadly support the proposal.

/ Posted 3rd July 2005

Terrorism

Over the life of sjhoward.co.uk, there have been major terrorist attacks including the London bombings, and we have seen radical new ways of tackling terrorism introduced – many at the expense of personal freedom.

Guantánamo prisoners return home today

Detention without trial is wrong.

I have yet to meet anyone who can make a convincing argument against the above statement. The right to a fair trial is a fundamental right of modern civilisation - and, for that matter, ancient civilisation too. So why, in the light of a few high profile terrorist attacks, are we denying people that right?

Don't misunderstand me here: The terrorist attacks on 11th September and other attacks worldwide have been terrible atrocities, but terrorism isn't new. Foreign terrorism is a fairly new concept to a young country like America, and it is a major step in the development of a nation. They must decide how to deal with such provocation, and this may well determine the future of their country as a whole. At the moment, I think they're taking the wrong path.

The Bush administration has violated more international laws at Guantánamo Bay than I can begin to count. The very fact that the American Constitution forbids this kind of treatment on American soil should put up some red flags. They have created a situation whereby the Presidential Administration could, if they wished to abuse the system, detain whoever they wanted and torture them. Is this really the foundation the American people want for their country? Is this not the very kind of Government that they tried to eliminate in Iraq?

I am in no way accusing Mr Bush of taking this kind of action. I'm confident that he is convinced that there is a need to detain these people, and that there are valid reasons in his eyes for not giving them proper trials. But we've seen the danger of this kind of approach in Iraq: Mr Blair had what he saw as high quality intelligence, which he trusted and believed, on the existence of Weapons of Mass Destruction in Iraq. He was wrong. What's to say Mr Bush isn't wrong? Isn't the fair trial the protection against this kind of error, just as publishing full information before a vote in the House of Commons is the protection against

Mr Blair's error? Just as Mr Blair failed to publish an authoritative Iraq dossier, Mr Bush is failing to provide trials for these people, and mistakes will inevitably be made.

As for the poor prisoners themselves, I cannot even imagine being locked in solitary confinement for three years. It would be mental torture, and would leave someone with lifelong mental trauma, and would probably have a similar impact on their families. Torture is completely wrong, and has no place in a modern society. The fact that these prisoners have been tortured, and the fact that the British Government has failed to condemn torture (by admitting evidence from torture in court, so long as it wasn't torture by British people) shows a deep problem in our society. Cracks of this magnitude in the very base of our society need patching up quickly, or it could lead to a serious collapse.

The news of four British detainees being released is clearly a welcome development, but we should be appalled at their detention rather than celebrating their release. How anyone expects that a society with such a loose moral grasp can ever hope to 'spread freedom' about the world, I just cannot begin to understand.

/ Posted 25th January 2005

Clarke announces anti-terror laws concession

My problem with the government's anti-terror plans as they stand, including the (unnecessary) proposed new legislation, is that it focuses on attacks *as they have happened in the past.*

If I were a terrorist (interesting concept - as someone who's not particularly religious, what would I be fighting for?), then I'd be thinking that huge terrorist attacks such as 9/11 and the Madrid train bombings have been done. People are already scared of these things, which (I would imagine) are difficult to co-ordinate, and potentially subject to being reasonably easily stopped if the plans are uncovered. So I wouldn't do that kind of attack.

Imagine instead the massive psychological damage which could be caused to nations across the globe if, for example, a series of comparatively minor attacks were co-ordinated to occur simultaneously in towns across the US and UK. Nobody would feel safe anywhere. It would be a massive psychological blow, and would also be relatively easier to co-ordinate. All that would need to be communicated to local operatives would be a chosen time and date, and then those operatives could simply plan something to happen at that time - even something as simple as arson or a small explosion, with no need for any illegal materials or specialist equipment or knowledge that might pick up a security service tracking. Imagine: Burning or exploding shopping malls, for example, across the small towns of the UK - those small towns where the people feel safest. That would cause true terror.

Of course, the problem with this idea is that extremist groups, by nature of their very extremity, would never be able to recruit enough people to make this the truly terrible event it could be. I suppose, due to the smaller nature of the area, the UK could be targeted in this way, but the US is just too big a place to recruit enough people to get the density of small-scale attacks which would be necessary.

So my problem here is that the UK Government seem insistent on protecting the big institutions, like Parliament and the capital as a whole, but that isn't where the greatest threat lies, because a massive and fundamentally more damaging attack than 9/11 could very easily be co-ordinated without raising many, if any, red flags with the security services. The Government need to think outside the box, and a law to allow people to be detained in their homes doesn't help that: Whilst it could stop a 9/11 style attack, it couldn't even begin to stop a terrorist attack such as that I've described. And, as we've seen on 9/11 through the transformation of passenger jets to effective guided missiles, the terrorists can be far more creative than the spooks.

/ Posted 22nd February 2005

What is an extremist?

The Guardian reports today that

> The government is to draw up a list of extremists from all over the world, the home secretary, Charles Clarke, announced as he revealed new anti-terrorism measures today.

My question is simple: How exactly does Mr Clarke propose to define an 'extremist'?

At first glance, the problem seems relatively easy, a simple case of including anyone who encourages others to kill themselves and others. But that ideology is more closely tied to religions around the world that you might expect - not just Islam, which this legislation is clearly unfairly aimed at, but also Christianity, the stated religion of choice for the majority of British citizens.

For example, a couple of weeks ago, I saw a Christian minister preaching about David and Goliath, effectively a story about a small unlikely minority overpowering and killing their perceived enemies of a much greater force. The minister went on to say that those that helped to fight this kind of injustice were truly treasured by her god. In the minds of the perverted minority, this could be taken as a sign that they, too, should fight to kill their perceived religious enemies, and go and blow up the nearest Mosque. In the minds of the potential bombers at least, the minister would have appeared to encourage them to take this course of action, and it is undeniable that this message can be taken from the sermon and from the Bible if that is what one is looking for. So does this minister count as an extremist?

Let's refer back to the Guardian article:

> The database would list individuals who had demonstrated 'unacceptable behaviour', which would include inflammatory preaching or running websites and writing articles intended to foment or provoke terrorism.

Ah. We've hit a bit of a brick wall. The database includes people who have demonstrated 'unacceptable behaviour'. That's helpful. But with the given examples including 'inflammatory preaching', I can't see any reason why our middle-of-the-road Christian minister couldn't be on the extremist database. Except, of course, for this small clause:

> He said the "unacceptable behaviour" would not be permitted by anyone with leave to enter or remain in this country, including students, asylum seekers and refugees.

So as long as our minister is British-born, it isn't an issue. If, however, early in life - perhaps too early to remember - she had fled with her parents from persecution in Zimbabwe, she could possibly end up on this database.

But ending up on this database - the purpose of which is sinisterly unexplained - is likely to be the least of our minister's worries, when she considers what else is in this upcoming legislation:

> He said the legislation would create three new criminal offences - acts preparatory to terrorism; indirect incitement to terrorism, which would cover those who glorified and condoned terror acts; and giving and receiving terrorist training.

This minister, in preaching what many thousands have preached before her, has undoubtedly given 'indirect incitement to terrorism'. She didn't mean to put the idea into the perverted minds of her audience, but she's managed to do it. That'll be a lengthy jail sentence for her, then.

Now I'm quite likely to be accused of being silly here. People will doubtless point out that this is not what the legislation is intended for. But - and here's something this government doesn't seem to understand - that doesn't matter.

Laws are not restricted to what they were meant to be used for. Judges and the police have a nasty habit of sticking to the very letter of the law. That's why laws have to be carefully constructed, debated, and re-written almost to destruction, and not rammed through Parliament to ensure as little opposition as possible.

If this government continues to make laws which are this full of gaping holes, sooner or later it's going to turn round and bite them back. For instance, when Tony Blair encourages us to do everything possible to defeat these terrorists, is he not indirectly inciting me to go and commit a terrorist attack on foreign soil, against those I perceive to have been behind the terrorist attack here?

These laws also leave the door open for a future, even less moral government to legitimately lock up their opposition - after all, speaking against the government must surely be indirect incitement to terrorism - and generally rule with an iron fist.

The government may well feel we're under a great terrorist threat, but much of their legislation designed to combat it puts us in ever greater danger of a future much more bleak than the very occasional terror attack. In short, they need to get a grip.

/ Posted 20th July 2005

Respond carefully to this abhorrent attack

Yesterday saw the biggest terrorist attack on London in many years, as four bombs killed dozens and injured hundreds. Television schedules were cleared as an apparent power surge on the London Underground turned into something much more sinister, and the roof was blown off a double-decker bus. The contrast between the mood in London today, and the mood 24 hours ago is palpable even to me, 200 miles away.

The BMA's building in Tavistock Square was left spattered with blood. An institution founded on the principle of helping the most needy made unclean in the name of a loving, caring religion. The G8, meeting to discuss action to be taken against many of the injustices Muslims try to fight, disrupted. Innocent bystanders killed, as specifically forbidden in the Koran. Is any further proof needed that 'religious extremist' is a misnomer? These people couldn't be further removed from the very religious principles they claim to defend. They aren't 'religious extremists' - they're amoral murders who sully the good name of the religion they claim to defend.

Yet to fight a 'war on terror' and actively engage in combat with these people is not helpful. To do so gives them a true cause to battle against. By simply defending ourselves from their attacks, and recovering as quickly as possible when they manage to strike, we stop pro-actively providing them with reasons to attack, and make their job of recruitment much harder. Curbing our own civil liberties through ill-thought-out legislation and restrictions on our daily lives only serves to give these people hope, and a sense of achievement, to further invigorate their disturbed cause.

Dozens of people have been unexpectedly - and almost inexplicably - bereaved in this attack, and my thoughts are with them. But it is crucial that these poor people hold firm, and stand united with the rest of London against the people who committed these atrocities; and however hard it is, that means not seeking vengeance against the religion or people they claim to represent, as these are as innocent as their loved ones.

Our government must also respond properly, with correct measure, and should not try and restrict our freedoms further. As high as is the human cost of this terrible tragedy, is freedom not worth so much more? This country has certainly paid a price many times higher on many occasions during our history. Of course we should defend our country, but not at any cost. To do so simply increases the perceived success of these terrorists.

/ Posted 8th July 2005

These bombers are to be condemned, but they're not evil

In the wake of the London bombings, one word seems to be resonating between much of the public, much of the media, and many politicians. That word is 'evil'. The attacks themselves were doubtlessly evil, but as far as I am concerned, the perpetrators were not.

To say that terrorists are evil is as illogical and irrational as saying bacteria are evil when they kill patients. Nobody would possibly trust a doctor who said that a patient was afflicted with 'evil', and we should no more trust politicians who insist on calling these bombers evil. To call them that suggests that they are an ever-present force which can never be truly and completely overcome, and immediately marks them out as 'different' from the rest of society, when the message to be taken away from the tragedy is that these young Muslims were not 'different' at all - they were normal young lads, cruelly brainwashed by expert criminals. As such, we should be viewing the radicalisation of young Muslims in this country as a major problem which needs to be tackled, not some mystical wicked force.

Many will have great difficulty in having sympathy with these killers, but it should be remembered that they are killing for irrational reasons which have been planted by expert criminals. And, what's more, society at large has contributed to their delusional fantasies by continually alienating the Muslim community. Every time we mention terrorists who claim to follow Islam they are branded 'Muslim terrorists'. Yet we would never dream of labelling the IRA 'Christian terrorists', or of characterising KKK lynchings as murders committed by 'Christian extremists'. Similarly, the religious background of Jewish, Sikh, or Hindu terrorists wouldn't even be worthy of mention.

Clearly, the mass media have succeeded in beginning to demonise one religion and heritage in the national conscience - and now, even our Prime Minister is refusing to come out unequivocally in support of the Muslim community. Is this not exactly what happened in Germany circa 1933, and exactly what millions later fought and lost their lives to avoid?

We should not be demonising a whole religion, and calling its members 'evil'. We should be tackling the extremists who are brain washing the young people of this country into killing themselves and others, and who are no more Muslim than William J Simmons was Christian. Perhaps I'm wrong, but if the bombers had been Christians called 'Joe Bloggs', 'John Smith', and 'James Jones', rather than being Muslims called 'Shehzad Tanweer', 'Hasib Mir Hussain', and 'Mohammed Sadique Khan', I think there would have been much more of national outcry against the people orchestrating the attacks, campaigns to educate young people against radicalisation, and - ultimately - a lot more sympathy for the bombers.

The real tragedy from these bombings is that we haven't learned the lessons. After the attacks, Muslims are more excluded than ever, and new anti-terror laws to be introduced will almost certainly end up being enforced more against Muslim communities, further alienating them, and increasing the opportunities for criminals to radicalise the young people of these communities. Effectively, the national response to this attack is doing little more than making future attacks more likely.

The London bombers are many things. But 'evil' is not one of them. And until we realise that, the situation becomes more grave by the day.

/ Posted 14th July 2005

Further London bombings

It's very difficult to comment on a situation like that in London, particularly when it is ongoing - even as I type, it would appear that an arrest has been made in Birmingham, and suspicious suitcases are being dealt with there. I would personally have thought that it can't be too difficult to track down failed suicide bombers - after all, they didn't expect to survive and so presumably wouldn't have put plans in place to get away.

It is clear that these attacks, and attempted attacks, are terrible. We can only hope that fewer will happen in future, though that looks increasingly unlikely. It is important in all of these to keep one's head, and I can only hope that the police haven't lost theirs, with the reports today of a horrific killing by police this morning at Stockwell tube station, which appears to me to have been an over-reaction to a perceived threat. The basic story is that a man under surveillance following the attacks refused to follow police orders, and so was shot five times at close range. I wasn't there, and can't claim to really know what went on, but I do wonder whether the situation was grave enough to use lethal action - and why was it necessary to shoot him *five times*? Perhaps the police were acting entirely professionally, as one would expect them to, but there are clearly questions which need to be addressed. We can't go killing every Asian man in a big coat who doesn't do as police ask.

In the two weeks since the 7th July attacks, there have been over 250 security alerts, and armed police officers are now stationed at every tube station and patrolling the streets. A second attack can only increase the fear, and it would appear that certainly American tourism is suffering. In other words, the terrorists appear to be succeeding in disrupting our daily lives, and - essentially - terrorising us. At the same time, it's not good enough for the police to simply instruct Londoners to 'get on with their normal life'. You can't instruct someone to not be scared.

As I've said, it's impossible to reflectively comment on an ongoing situation - and it appears that this situation will be ongoing for some considerable time - and I have no solutions to the problems I've mentioned, but I'm sure I'll post more about this in future.

/ Posted 22nd July 2005

War

Following each of the terrorist attacks of the last few years, including that of two weeks ago in London, George Bush, Tony Blair, and their associated administrations and political parties have roundly criticised the terrible jihad - deliberately mistranslated as 'Holy war' - which radicalised Muslim groups have declared against Western society. They conveniently seem to forget that it is not the radical groups which declared the war, but George Bush, when he declared a War on Terror.

According to my dictionary, war is

> the waging of armed conflict against an enemy

Conflict. That involves retaliation. It's a two-way thing. So how can our leaders declare a war, effectively beginning a two-sided conflict, and then condemn any attacks which come their way? They've said they are attacking their enemy, the enemy is providing a great deal less retaliation that the force which the coalition is putting forward.

Can one imagine Churchill standing up and spouting about how it's terrible that fifty British citizens should die in the war, when we've killed tens of thousands of innocent people in their home countries? Tony Blair and George Bush have announced that this is a war. They have to expect collateral damage on both sides, since that is a product of war. If they weren't comfortable with that idea - and remain uncomfortable with it - then why declare war in the first place?

/ Posted 23rd July 2005

The intelligence question and conspiracy theories

Last Friday, with reference to the London bombings, Sir Ian Blair (the Metropolitan Police commissioner) announced that no warning of an attack had been given to the police by any organisation whatsoever.

On Monday, Mr Blair announced that

> I know of no intelligence specific enough to have allowed them to prevent last Thursday's attacks.

This implies, of course, that there was *some* intelligence suggesting an attack. Intelligence that the police clearly weren't made aware of, and so clearly weren't investigating. Why not?

On BBC Radio Five Live, a former Scotland Yard official, Peter Power, confirmed that an exercise simulating the exact nature of this attack was underway as the attack actually happened:

> At half past nine this morning we were actually running an exercise for a company of over a thousand people in London based on simultaneous bombs going off precisely at the railway stations where it happened this morning

Of course, this is particularly intriguing because at the time the interview was conducted, it was thought that the bombs had detonated over a period of about an hour. It has only recently transpired that the bombs detonated simultaneously.

I'm not one for conspiracy theories. I'm not about to suggest that this was all planned by the government for some largely unconvincing reason. But it suggests to me that intelligence *was* received, specific about the threat but not specific on time - and hence not a 'warning' - it could have happened hours, days, weeks, months, or years after the intelligence was received.

The security service, or possibly the government, were therefore possibly getting together lots of discussions of the type Power attended, to discuss whether the planned responses would be appropriate, and whether any extra security measures could be implemented. This would certainly not be an unprecedented measure - procedures are usually reviewed in the light of a given threat. The fact that one of these meetings happened to coincide with the attack itself is just coincidence.

This would also explain why Mr Blair is refusing an investigation into the intelligence failures - the intelligence services were actually quite good, as many of the details about the attack were known. Mr Blair would obviously prefer that this weren't known, though, because it would appear that despite knowing of the attack, they were unable to stop it. Which is true, but obviously these situations are rather more tricky - one can't close the whole underground for years on the basis of possible threats… it would never be open!

Whether Al-Qaeda or another group are behind the attack or not, I have no idea, and haven't really seen any convincing evidence either way. The fact that the bombers' identities have been found so quickly, though, apparently linking them to Al-Qaeda, makes me wonder whether the attacks were orchestrated by a group unconnected to them but attempting to provoke reprisal attacks against Muslim groups in the UK. But I might be reading too much into that.

/ Posted 13th July 2005

Blair to face charges over Stockwell?

Yesterday's *Observer* splashed on the story that Sir Ian Blair could face charges over the killing of Jean Charles de Menezes on 21st July last year, based on the fact that the Crown Prosecution Service's analysis of events focuses on Sir Ian and two other senior commanders. This is, of course, in addition to the ongoing inquiry as to whether Sir Ian misled the public in the aftermath of the attacks of 7th July. And, one year on, it would appear that suspects are still being shot without warning.

Now, I'm fairly certain that Sir Ian has acted wrongly at various points in the aftermath of 7th July, but I don't think he's done so knowingly, and I don't think he's deliberately set out to cause harm and mislead the public. I don't think that charging him with any kind of offence is going to serve a great purpose here. He should have resigned, as he's at least nominally in charge of officers who killed an innocent man, but I don't think that can be blamed on him *per se*.

It would appear to uniformed me that what's going on here is that too many police are being handed guns with too little training and too much emotion. The government is all too keen to get armed police on the streets so that it looks like they're doing something in the face of an apparent terrorist threat and this results in armed officers needing to be trained quickly, churning out like sausages in a sausage factory. But I wouldn't want to be confronted by a sausage with a gun: If police are going to carry guns, they should be very highly trained, not just in how to use them, but more importantly in how and when *not* to use them.

It seems to me that such training either isn't happening, or isn't sufficient. Charging Sir Ian Blair with health and safety offences for failing in his duty of care won't change that. A change in police and government culture - rather more difficult to achieve - just might.

/ Posted 5th June 2006

Deport me now

Charles Clarke's new terror plans scare me. Let's look at just one of the new powers:

> Home secretary automatically to consider deporting any foreigner involved in listed extremist bookshops, centres, organisations and websites

The Government wants to have the power to deport any foreigner who it considers 'extreme'. I can't begin to believe that any government would even suggest such measures - how can anyone seriously think that a government has the right to deport those who, essentially, it disagrees with? And, just to clarify, Mr Blair has already made it quite plain that we're not solely talking about bombers and murderers:

> We are dealing not with an isolated criminal act but with an extreme and evil ideology

This government wants to legislate against *an ideology*, not just the crimes which might stem from that ideology. Not only that, but we're now allowing our politicians to use judgement laden words like 'evil' to describe sets of people - that's just wrong, and further alienates the sizeable Muslim minority with sympathetic views. In fact, it doesn't just indirectly alienate them, it actively does it:

> Make justifying or glorifying terrorism anywhere an offence

If I sit here and try and understand the rationale behind terrorist attacks, and try to draw conclusions about how it is justified in the minds of the terrorists, I'm breaking the law. We're being asked to continue an ill-defined 'war' against an enemy we're forbidden to try and understand. Surely that kind of thing shouldn't happen in a healthy democratic society? And whatever happened to free speech?

I've previously said that we're bordering on the political situation of Germany circa 1933, and the semantics are getting ever close: Hitler branded large groups of people (most noticeably the leaders of Czechoslovakia) as evil terrorists.

Besides which, in the age of global communication, does it really matter if the people attempting to incite terrorism are in a different country? The suspected nine-eleven hijackers were allegedly indoctrinated in Afghanistan, and that didn't seem to harm the scale of their attack.

This is bad, dangerous, and unnecessary legislation which restricts our freedoms - including our freedom of thought - even more than ever before, and should be strongly opposed.

/ Posted 24th August 2005

Blair, Wolfgang, and terror laws

As no-one can fail to have noticed, earlier this week, 82-year-old long-term Labour supporter and Conference-goer Walter Wolfgang was physically removed from the Conference centre by 'heavies' after shouting the single word 'nonsense' during Jack Straw's speech. The police then detained him under Anti-Terror Legislation when he later tried to re-enter the hall.

This gentleman clearly posed no terrorist threat. His only 'crime' was to utter a single word when the Labour bigwigs didn't want him to. And yet he was held under the 'crucial' Terror Laws that we were assured would only be used in the most extreme circumstances to detain the most dangerous people.

For some time, people including myself have been arguing that

> Laws [cannot be] restricted to what they were meant to be used for. Judges and the police have a nasty habit of sticking to the very letter of the law ... If this government continues to make laws which are this full of gaping holes, sooner or later it's going to turn round and bite them back.

And yet, in the face of police blatantly flouting Mr Blair's publicly stated intentions for the laws, all he's done is apologise to Mr Wolfgang. He's not revisiting this legislation, and he's not even disciplining the police force. In fact, Mr Blair wants to *extend* the powers available to the police. And all because he, in his infinite wisdom, has bypassed thousands of years of history and declared that protection of the common-man is now more important than the freedom of the innocent. The logical conclusion of which is surely that we just lock up - or kill - everyone who we don't like the look of.

The terrorist threat to this country may be different to that which we have faced in the past, but it's no so great that we should sacrifice the central tenet of our justice system and beliefs. If we change something so fundamental with so little thought and debate, then what is left to protect?

/ Posted 1st October 2005

The new terror alert system in full

You may remember from last week that a new terror alerts system is to be introduced in response to the London bombing of 7th July. Clearly, it's important that the public know the terror level at all times, because if we'd known that it was *lowered* from 'severe' to 'substantial' just before the attacks then we would've been more vigilant. Apparently. No, I don't understand either.

Anyway, the new system does away with 'Negligible', because, durr, we're always facing the biggest threat we've ever faced - otherwise we wouldn't vote for policies which restrict our everyday lives (like ID cards or House Arrest). They've also combined 'Severe Defined' and 'Severe General' into 'Severe', because we can never be sure whether we've received intelligence about an attack anyway until after the attack takes place. And no-one really knows whether the intelligence is 'patchy' or 'clear and authoritative' anyway.

So how will the new system work? Well, I reckon the levels of threat will be determined much like this:

Low: Oh my god, there's a terrorist with a big nuclear bomb sat with a detonator in the centre of London. Best not panic the public, let's keep the alert level down.

Moderate: Hmm, some planes seem to be heading off course and towards some tall public buildings. Probably not worth calming the public completely, they might not accept draconian control measures, but let's reassure them a bit.

Substantial: The Daily Mail, that most reliable intelligence source, says someone who once passed Prince Charles's butler's cousin twice removed on Oxford Street made a comment that the Monarchy should be abolished! Clearly a terrorist plotting to kill the Queen!

Severe: Someone seen calmly walking into a tube station wearing a light denim jacket. *Shoot!*

Critical: Save our good Christian souls, a Muslim family has moved into a quaint village in Middle England! We don't want *those people* here! *Deport them!*

So there you go! In fact, the *official* definitions are worse:

Low: 'An attack is unlikely' - Which presumably means it's not likely, but it is possible. See also 'moderate'.

Moderate: 'An attack is possible but not likely' - Which presumably means an attack is, erm, unlikely. See also 'low'.

Substantial: 'Strong possibility of an attack' - Presumably meaning an attack is quite likely. See also 'severe'.

Severe: 'An attack is highly likely' - Or, there is a strong possibility of an attack. See also 'substantial'.

Critical: 'An attack is expected imminently' - But we're not going to tell you where or when. *Bwwaaaahaahaaa!*

I feel safer already!

/ Posted 20th July 2006

Iraq

Mr Blair's war in Iraq will be considered the defining feature of his Premiership for many years to come. In common with most of the population, I agreed with neither the war itself nor the bungled way in which it has been conducted. I think that's made quite clear in this selection of posts.

Kenneth Bigley

I know that it's probably poor timing to start ranting about the latest terrible events in Iraq already, but I think that this really needs to be said.

Almost all of the vox-pops and people I've spoken to have said that we shouldn't negotiate with terrorists, even with these potential grim outcomes. That's a very commendable sentiment, but completely irrelevant. The current situation should not ever have involved either Bush or Blair, let alone left them appearing to need to negotiate with terrorists.

The position of the Iraqi government is clear. They want to release the women in Iraqi prisons, so that the views of all of those Iraqis (and there are more than a few) who think that the imprisonment of women is wrong are represented. Indeed, they see all Iraqis as valid citizens, so that a government can be formed which represents the views of all Iraqis. This is also what the people holding Ken Bigley want.

The spanner in the works that has directly led to the deaths of two US Citizens, and possibly one British citizen, is George W Bush. The two women that Mr Bigley's captors want to see released are in US custody, supposedly on behalf of the Iraqi government. How sovereign can the Iraqi government be if their wishes are being ignored? Of course, George Bush doesn't want to be accused of letting Saddam's friends go. But, crucially, it isn't his call. It's nothing to do with him, and I'm fairly sure that what he is doing breaks international law.

And Tony Blair is left in the middle. Well, actually, I'm not entirely sure of Tony's stance, but it seems to me that Jack Straw is aware that this situation is incredibly unjust, and it's an arrogant US President that will effectively kill a British citizen.

This isn't some kind of hidden story. It's been played out in full on the 'better' TV news programmes, and in the broadsheets. But the country doesn't seem to be getting the message, which suggests that the tabloid newspapers and programmes are over-simplifying the story. Lucky for Blair.

Tony Blair should publicly call for President Bush to but out of Iraq's affairs. But, of course, he would never do that, especially when it's his good friend's election year.

Not that Tony's much better - and this bit's purely my opinion, and if it's complete bollocks then that's my bad - but why has Mr Blair brought up the hunting debate now? Because it's a very devisive issue, bound to cause protest at his Party Conference. So the news will be full of protestors who support fox-hunting - approximately half of the viewers will disagree with what these protesters are saying, and hence this won't be nearly as damaging as if Mr Blair had been faced with hordes of War in Iraq protestors - who would inevitably have grabbed the headlines has it not been for this policy suddenly making a reappearance - with whom the majority of the viewers would sympathise.

/ Posted 23rd September 2004

Attorney General: Before and after

When trying to decide what exactly the document Lord Goldsmith produced and put before the House of Commons before the vote on the War in Iraq actually was (particularly in terms of whether it was supposed to be representative of the advice he gave as a whole), it would seem sensible to consult it's author directly. Not surprisingly, when the *Daily Telegraph* interviewed him earlier this week they did, and received the following response:

> I never said it was a summary.

Except, if we flip back to November 2003 in Hansard, then he was, erm, saying it was a summary:

> This statement was a summary of my view of the legal position

So he *did* say it was a summary, whether he likes it or not.

To provide you with a summary of my own: When the full document was secret, his document *was* a summary; Once the full text was released and everyone could compare, it suddenly *wasn't* a summary. Funny, that.

We know that the Blair government likes massaging the facts a little, but here he's on record as directly contradicting himself. He's absolutely doubtlessly proven as lying. Yet, far from resigning, he hasn't even been sent out into the frenzied world of the media to apologise, or even clarify his comments. And all of this from a government which promised to be 'whiter than white'.

If we were observing a developing nation with a government that was lying about the process of deciding about launching an internationally condemned war, not only would we have a few nasty things to say about said government, but there would be those in our government who would want military action taken against it. And yet when it's people in their own government doing it, they don't seem to mind quite as much. Talk about double-standards.

/ Posted 28th May 2005

Newsweek's 'lasting damage'

Anybody who follows the news will know that *Newsweek* recently made the slightly absurd claim that a soldier at Guantanamo Bay had flushed the Koran down the toilet. Clearly, they didn't think through the physics of the situation, and evidently later had to retract the story. The official White House line was that *Newsweek* had done 'lasting damage' to the US image in the Muslim world. Given that the Pentagon have now released details of incidents at Guantanamo Bay where guards kicked, wrote obscenities in, and threw water and splashed urine on copies of the Koran, this frankly makes the White House look plainly and openly vindictive.

Before condemning *Newsweek*, the White House must surely have looked into the case to confirm it wasn't true. And in the course of that investigation, these other incidents must surely have cropped up. And yet the White House has the audacity to condemn not the soldiers who have abused the Koran, and by association the Muslim world as a whole, but *Newsweek*. Even though the central message of the story - that the Koran was being mishandled - was effectively true. It's not even that difficult to see that the ideas of covering something in urine and that of flushing it down the toilet are not that far removed from each other, and could easily become confused in translation.

The *Newsweek* story caused riots across the Muslim world, and thus indirectly led to the deaths of at least fifteen people in Afghanistan. Does the White House really believe that these people were protesting because of the particular details of the *Newsweek* story, or does it believe that the riots were caused by the US's lack of respect for other cultures? Or does the White House no longer hold any true beliefs, other than belief in the supremacy of the US and US citizens?

Of course, this action is not a million miles removed from our own Andrew Gilligan incident, whereby he reported that the Dodgy Dossier had been 'sexed up'. Effectively, it had. And yet, for tripping up on the details - in this case, misrepresenting the position of David Kelly - Gilligan and the Beeb were condemned. Yet the story was basically true.

Is it right that administrations should cover their embarrassments by ridiculing the relatively minor errors of others? The argument can be made that the media are forever condemning politicians for minor slips and lexical errors. But, in my mind at least, this does not mean that they can do the same to the media. Politicians, whether they like it or not, are quite rightly held to a higher standard. They have to prove to us that they are worthy of leading the country, and that they have the moral standing necessary to lead a country morally. To refuse to admit to a wider problem because of small errors in accusations - indeed, to ridicule the person who made those accusations - is neither moral nor open.

And to think, politicians wonder why the public don't trust them.

/ Posted 4th June 2005

The Chatham House report

Chatham House has published a report whose conclusion is, in a nutshell…

> There is no doubt that the situation over Iraq has imposed particular difficulties for the UK, and for the wider coalition against terrorism... The UK is at particular risk because it is the closest ally of the United States.

Jack Straw and Tony Blair, who have published precisely zero reports into this, are absolutely convinced that Chatham House is wrong:

> 'I'm astonished that Chatham House is now saying that we should not have stood shoulder to shoulder with our long-standing allies in the United States,' Mr Straw told reporters before chairing an EU foreign ministers meeting in Brussels.
>
> 'The time for excuses for terrorism is over,' he said. 'The terrorists have struck across the world, in countries allied with the United States, backing the war in Iraq and in countries which had nothing whatever to do with the war in Iraq.'

Of course, he's very helpfully misrepresented the contents of the report, which does not say that the UK should not have supported the USA, and also does not say that if we had not done so, there would be no terrorist attacks. The report merely suggests that antagonising terror cells increases the chance of a terror attack occurring. Which, logic says, it does.

Whilst terror cells are quite happy to attack many places in the Western world in order to make their voices heard, they are doubtlessly going to expend greater efforts attacking the countries which most greatly represent the ideology which they wish to attack. And if this country is attacking Muslims around the world, logic follows that we're going to be somewhere near the top of the list. If we weren't attacking them, we'd probably be a little lower down.

It's also interesting to see today that Charles Clarke has decided that his 'crucial' new terror laws, which he claims are necessary to secure the country and help prevent further attacks like those in London, are now to be introduced only in December, because our hard-working MPs need a summer holiday, and really can't be expected to stay back for an extra couple of weeks. If Charles Clarke continues to say that these laws are so 'crucial' after the summer, then I hope someone will point out to him that his own government have delayed their introduction twice - once by calling an early General Election, and once by refusing a summer recall - and so they really can't be that important.

As serious a story as this is, I think there's room for a little humour. *The Times* provides this for us, with possibly the most ridiculous heading for a newspaper graphic so far this year: 'Tentacles of Terror'. Whoever said *The Times* was becoming more tabloidesque?

In all seriousness, Mr Blair and his government must begin to accept that their foreign policy has an impact at home as well as abroad. Until they do this, the country will be in much greater danger than is truly necessary.

/ Posted 18th July 2005

The Chatham argument continues

Following yesterday's publication of the Chatham House report, which was swiftly followed by mildly ridiculous denials by Tony Blair, Jack Straw, Charles Clarke, and John Reid, an argument is understandably being fought between the media and the government. The government is losing.

Shortly before the London bombings, an intelligence report claimed that

> Events in Iraq are continuing to act as motivation and a focus of a range of terrorist-related activity in the UK

Mr Blair's denials of this demonstrate that he is not accepting what his intelligence sources are telling him. He'd prefer to spin his own version, which doesn't get him in quite such hot political water.

Now in the face of overwhelming logic, Mr Blair has apparently seen fit to shift his argument slightly.

> 'Of course these terrorists will use Iraq as an excuse as they will Afghanistan. But 9/11 happened before both to those and before then the excuse was US policy.
>
> 'They will always have their reasons for acting. We have to be really careful to giving into the perverted and twisted logic to which they argue.'
>
> He said compromising on certain aspects of foreign policy would not make the terrorists go away but would enable them to argue that the UK 'was on the run, let's step it up'.

So he appears to no longer be arguing against the obvious point that attacking Iraq has provided terrorists with another 'excuse' for attacking us, and thus provided yet another reason, increasing the risk to the country. The third paragraph of the above quotation also shows very clearly that he's now admitting that British foreign policy affects the actions of terrorists, something that he's previously strenuously denied. So that's quite a significant shift, however subtly he's tried to make it.

In a slightly pointless exercise, the *Guardian* has conducted a poll which concluded that two-thirds of Britons believe that there is a link between the invasion of Iraq and the London bombings, and over half believe that Mr Blair bears some responsibility for the bombings. The value of these particular results is not really very clear, but tucked away at the bottom is a much more significant statistic: Support for ID cards has fallen, relative to polls taken both immediately after the bombings, and - crucially - before them. So, even in the face of a terrorist attack on British soil, ID card support is falling. This is particularly significant, because one of the central arguments earlier in Mr Blair's ID cards campaign was that after any hypothetical terrorist attack, people would be angry that he had not done any more to protect them, and would not be worrying about civil liberties arguments. This has today clearly been proven to be a flawed argument.

All things considered, it would seem that the Chatham House report has played badly for the Prime Minister. But, more frustratingly, it never needed to, if only he'd accepted in the first place that foreign policy affects the terrorism risk. If handled correctly, this admission would have been much less politically damaging than this Chatham House report appears to have been, as the report has essentially made him look pretty stupid, and their handling of the attack as a whole hasn't really helped their terrorism policies. But then, it's very easy to say these things with hindsight, and I'm sure that when trying to deal with a terrorist attack of this nature, life is rather more difficult. Unless, of course, you've got a well thought out plan. But this government isn't really very good at planning for unexpected events, is it? Look at Iraq!

Oh, and just to make you feel extra safe, the leaked report also concluded that

> At present, there is not a group with both the current intent and the capability to attack the UK.

Our lives, their hands.

/ Posted 19th July 2005

Iraq: Three years on

Last Tuesday, a little more than three years after the first strikes against Iraq, Mr Blair gave a foreign policy speech. I'm not one for deconstructing speeches at great length, but he has said a few things I disagree with.

> the defining characteristic of today's world is its interdependence

That, to be frank, is bollocks. Mr Blair isn't interested in interdependence. In fact, he want to *lose* the interdependence that's been foisted upon him, as he doesn't want to have to rely on other countries for supplies of, well, anything - least of all, oil. And in many ways, that's sound foreign policy. The world is an unpredictable place, you can never be sure that your friends today will be your friends tomorrow. So to start waffling on about 'common global policy based on common values' is utter rot. The peoples of the world are never going to have common values. People are always going to think different things; the challenge is to live alongside one another, not to try and make everybody adhere to the same 'common values'.

He says we shouldn't 'extremism, conflict or injustice go unchecked'. Whose extremist, whose conflict, and whose injustice? We don't have 'common values'. One man's extremist is another's moderate. And if we're not letting conflict go unchecked, who's checking up on the Iraq war? And what's injustice? There's plenty of that in this country. Our value system says that treating the poor worse than the rich is less terrible than treating women worse than men. Perhaps those in the Middle East disagree. That doesn't mean we should carpet bomb them, it means we should discuss (celebrate?) our differences.

> The consequence of this thesis is a policy ... that is active not reactive.

We're now admitting to bombing countries based on what they might do in the future. Whatever happened to that one 'common value' of innocent until proven guilty?

> This world view - which I would characterise as a doctrine of benign inactivity - sits in the commentator's seat, almost as a matter of principle.

Would we not rather benign inactivity than malignant activity, the logical conclusion of which is a world permanently at war?

> The easiest line for any politician seeking office in the West today is to attack American policy. A couple of weeks ago as I was addressing young Slovak students, one got up, denouncing US/UK policy in Iraq, fully bought in to the demonisation of the US, utterly oblivious to the fact that without the US and the liberation of his country, he would have been unable to ask such a question, let alone get an answer to it.

And, perhaps, if we in this country had this 'pro-active' stance whereby we attack anyone we don't feel quite fits into the ideals and values we hold true to ourselves, then Mr Blair may not have been able to mock such a student. Attacking a country provokes a response from that country and its allies. Hitler learned that around about 1935, when he decided that Poland didn't quite fit into his world vision. When will Blair realise it? When will it 'click' for him that 'pro-active' warfare is nothing short of a race to world instability? And why does he feel he can engage in such activity, and yet roundly denounce similar action in the Israel - Palestine conflict?

> Ministers have been advised never to use the term 'Islamist extremist'. It will give offence. It is true. It will. There are those - perfectly decent-minded people - who say the extremists who commit these acts of terrorism are not true Muslims. And, of course, they are right. They are no more proper Muslims than the Protestant bigot who murders a Catholic in Northern Ireland is a proper Christian. But, unfortunately, he is still a 'Protestant' bigot. To say his religion is irrelevant is both completely to misunderstand his motive and to refuse to face up to the strain of extremism within his religion that has given rise to it.

Yes, but you would call him 'Protestant', not 'Christian'. Just as the KKK were the KKK, and not 'Christian'. Why, then, associate a whole religion with the terrorists rather than being more specific? The answer is straightforward: The majority of the electorate identify with Christian values, and so to attack Christianity is to attack the electorate. Only a minority identify with Muslim values, and it's politically convenient to associate a religion with the cause, rather than to deal with the underlying issues. You would never class the actions of that Northern Ireland Protestant as religious, but rather as political. To class the actions of Muslims as political gives them a degree of validity, which means they have to be argued against and tackled. That's hard. Much easier to say 'Muslim bad', and demonise the set of people, then the majority, believing as they are told to believe, will support any action against 'the baddies'.

> I recall the video footage of Mohammed Sadiq Khan, the man who was the ringleader of the 7/7 bombers. ... There was something tragic, terrible but also ridiculous about such a diatribe. He may have been born here. But his ideology wasn't. And that is why it has to be taken on, everywhere.

But by 'taking it on', Mr Blair means criminalising it, killing it. Not reasoning with it. Not arguing the points on their merits. Is it wrong to say that the West persecutes Muslims? No, there's evidence of it in the newspapers most days. Is the right response to attack Britain? No. But does that mean we should simply destroy the West-hating ideology, or that we should rather engage with it, tackle the issues, and move forward?

> This terrorism will not be defeated until its ideas, the poison that warps the minds of its adherents, are confronted, head-on, in their essence, at their core.

Yes! Yes! Yes!

> I mean telling them their attitude to America is absurd; their concept of governance pre-feudal; their positions on women and other faiths, reactionary and regressive;

No! No! No! You don't 'defeat ideas' by *telling* people that they're wrong. You explain to them. You let them make their argument, and you engage with it, recognise the kernel truths, and point out the flaws. Terrorists *know* Mr Blair finds their beliefs abhorrent - that's the *raison d'etre* behind their terrorism. How's that approach going so far?

> **It is the age-old battle between progress and reaction, between those who embrace and see opportunity in the modern world and those who reject its existence; between optimism and hope on the one hand; and pessimism and fear on the other.**

This just returns to the original point: Why should all the world be the same? Why can't we have some nations we would view as 'progressive', and some we wouldn't? Who are we to cast judgement over the beliefs and values of those so far removed from ourselves?

Anyway, enough from Blair. A couple of Grauniad folks have had their say on the speech, and they know rather more about these things than I. Dan Plesch, like me, thinks he's wrong. Harry Hatchet thinks he's right. Perhaps I'm wrong, and Harry's right. I'm really in no position to judge.

But something that's clear to me is that this is all political bickering. It's undoubtedly essential bickering, deciding the future foreign policy of the country, but, as with most policies in politics, it'll be changed by this time next year. One thing that won't change is the reality of the situation for people who've lived it. For them, Iraq isn't a three-year problem, it's a thirty-year one.

/ Posted 26th March 2006

Saddam Hussein has been executed

Breaking news in the last few minutes that a 71 year-old grandfather has been filmed being barbarically killed using an ancient method of state killing after a highly criticised show trial in an unstable country. This is, apparently, 'justice'.

/ Posted 30th December 2006

European Politics

European politics tends to get very little press in the UK, but with the possibility of the introduction of a European Constitution, Europhobic coverage increased somewhat – and not least on my site.

More crazy frogs on TV…

…as the French go to the polls in their referendum on the EU Constitution. My jokes never improve on this site, do they?

For all the coverage of the vote in today's Sundays, there seems little point in commenting until the decision is made and announced. But, hey, this is a comment site so I feel somewhat obliged. The *Guardian* website has published a 7pm update, as most of the polls across France close. It looks fairly clear that this is going to be a 'Non' vote, unless everyone has followed this voter's lead:

> Katia Volman, a 22-year-old student, left her ballot blank, saying the issues were too complicated to fully digest. 'I had so many reasons to vote yes or no so I left it blank and that way I won't regret my decision two days later,' she said.

Shortly afterwards, she returned herself to her usual wooden box, which she locks herself in night and day, claiming that the world is too complicated and she doesn't want to do anything in life that she might later regret. The reason being that she wants Edith Piaf singing 'Je ne regrette rein' at her funeral. Or perhaps I'm just being cruel.

The *Independent on Sunday* says much the same thing; the *Telegraph* manages to write a full article on the referendum without mentioning Tony Blair, which is fairly impressive, even in their Q&A about what will happen if the French vote 'Non'. At the other end of the spectrum, the first word in the *Times*' article is 'BRITAIN'.

Other newspaper websites lead on clearly much more important stories than the future of Europe: 'Has Cilla been jilted for a young blonde?' - *The Mail*; 'Posh and Becks [sic] bubbly boozathon' - *The Mirror*; and 'Huntley's devil woman' - *The Sun*.

I also nearly forgot to mention that the *Guardian* has a rather exciting game on its website, to explain the various different possible outcomes of the referendum, on it's website. Exciting, of course, if you like that sort of thing. Which I'm not ashamed to admit I do. Well, a little bit ashamed, I guess.

/ Posted 29th May 2005

The man from Paris: He say 'Non!'

With fifty-five percent of the French voters giving the EU Constitution the thumbs down, many of today's papers are using words like 'crisis', 'confusion' and 'fear' today. There's even talk of 'huge' margins, which seems a bit over the top. Even the *Independent*, which declared on Saturday 'The significance of this poll lies in the campaign, not the result', gets its knickers in a bit of a twist. Though it does seem to accept the result of this referendum, unlike Tony Blair's victory in the General Election. Nobody seems to even mention the 70 percent turnout, and ask what it is we could learn from this. If we Brits have a referendum, I'd be surprised if fifty percent of voters bother to vote.

The *Guardian* has Europe stunned by the result, and its website has Tony Blair calling for a time of reflection. This combination makes it sound rather like somebody's died. They even seem to be progressing through the various stages of grief: We've had denial all this week, while they've been clinging on to the hope that a 'Yes' vote might just happen, and today we appear to have moved on to anger:

> France's 'no' is highly damaging to the credibility and popularity of the EU, already in very poor shape as shown by the record low turnout in the European elections last summer.

You evil French people… You've let the EU down, you've let Chirac down, but most of all you've let yourselves down.

The *Telegraph* is obviously pleased that the vote has gone its way, and they've done the predictable thing of printing a picture of a smiling Chirac casting his ballot.

The *Mail*'s position can be summed up by saying that it's the fifth headline on their website, just below 'Rod's daughter steps out with stepmum's ex' and two Big Brother headlines. Despite the fact that today's print edition says Big Brother has 'reached new levels of debauchery'.

So what does all this mean for the future of the Constitution? Well, pretty much what we've all known for weeks. It's not going to get very far without some redrafting. Which is incredibly predictable: You won't get hundreds of millions of people of different countries and cultures to agree to a 400-page document easily. And, to be perfectly honest, I'd be surprised to see it happen at all.

It's clear to anybody that the EU isn't working, and is in need of reform. But the reason it isn't working is because it's tried to become something it never intended to be in the first place - so the foundations are not appropriate. And to wait until there are twenty-five members and then try and negotiate a new set of firmer foundations seems rather silly. Yet this is the situation in which we find ourselves, and there's not an awful lot that can be done to change the past.

So, where do we go from here? I don't know. It would be impossible for the EU to break up completely, because some of the bonds are too strong. Piecemeal reform of existing agreements wouldn't solve the overall problem. So it looks like we're stuck with what we've got for now, with all of its quirks and inconsistencies. The existing treaties may not be a practical way to manage the newly enlarged EU, but, at the end of the day, when has European politics *ever* been straightforward and practical?

/ Posted 30th May 2005

The man from Amsterdam: He say 'Nee!'

Just days after the French rejected the EU Constitution, the Dutch have done the same. Not that it was much of a surprise. Mr Juncker, President of the EU, is obviously not happy. The Beeb says

> Mr Juncker seemed so distressed that he could hardly take in the fact of the second 'No' vote. The mood in Brussels is deep gloom.

I've never really imagined Brussels as a happy place anyway. But maybe that's just me.

Last time I wrote about this, when the French rejected the Constitution, I couldn't come up with a viable solution to get around this impasse. Now I've come up with one. And it's remarkably simple: Separate out the Constitution from the Treaty. Make the Constitution a short statement of self-evident rights and truths - which one would expect to be in a Constitution - and then have a separate treaty with all the legal eagle stuff in it. Then you can treat the Treaty as a Treaty, reforming it and remolding it over time until you eventually find the right mix, and the Constitution should sail through and easily be ratified by all twenty-five countries.

To the papers… The *Guardian* still appears to be mourning the loss, though it's overcome its initial anger: 'Crushing defeat leaves EU vision in tatters'; it also appears to think we're 'facing the prospect of a protracted period of recrimination, conflict and crisis'; The *FT* is somewhat less emotional: 'Europe in turmoil as the Dutch vote No'.

Judging by the state of the *Guardian*, you'd expect the *Independent* to be in floods - and yet. whilst it's clearly not happy ('The Netherlands has delivered a crushing 'no' vote on the European Constitution and plunged the EU into a crisis of confidence unprecedented in almost five decades of European integration'), it does at least seem to be looking forward, rather than excessively wailing over spilt milk.

I'm really quite surprised at the *Guardian*'s reaction to all of this, and for the first time in a long while feel slightly alienated by it. I don't think I've ever seen this degree of apparent grief, bordering on depression, from a national newspaper - and particularly not the *Guardian*. It's so far gone that it's bordering on parody - I almost expect to see the Constitution get a full page obituary.

So where will things go from here? It's hard to say, because this is European politics, in which logic seems to play no part. After a brief period of depression, the politicians will just have to regroup and see where they can take us. They'll probably try redrafting a bit, and trying to get it past the countries again. And failing. And then they'll have to do something pro-active, like reconsider the need for a Constitution and what should be in it. And then we might just get somewhere.

/ Posted 2nd June 2005

The man from Luxembourg: He say 'Jo!/Ja!/Oui!'

Three official languages? That ruins the meter my nicely clichéd title. The French and Dutch were more considerate.

But anyway, the point of this post is that the good people of Luxembourg have voted 'yes', by a relatively narrow margin, to the EU Constitution. Despite the fact that it's almost certainly dead. But, you know, good for them.

But if they have three official languages, and voting is compulsory, that must make one heck of a complicated ballot paper, because surely all three languages must be used so as not to disenfranchise anyone if it's compulsory. Unless they have three sets of papers, and then you have to request one in your chosen language. It's a conundrum. Any readers from Luxembourg who can clarify?

/ Posted 10th July 2005

The G8

In 2005, the annual G8 summit was held in the United Kingdom, and thus got much more coverage than usual. Large sections of the electorate were also exerting great pressure on the G8 to help to alleviate world debt, and the country as a whole was waiting with baited breath for their response. Attention was suddenly diverted, though, as the London bombings occurred half way through the summit, changing the mood of the nation absolutely.

The G8 and alleviating world debt

Gordon Brown, in a very Prime Ministerial speech, today announced that the G8 finance ministers have agreed, subject to conditions, to wipe out 100% of the debt owed by eighteen countries with immediate effect. Those countries are Benin, Bolivia, Burkina Faso, Ethiopia, Ghana, Guyana, Honduras, Madagascar, Mali, Mauritania, Mozambique, Nicaragua, Niger, Rwanda, Senegal, Tanzania, Uganda, and Zambia. A further nine (Cameroon, Chad, Democratic Republic of Congo, Gambia, Guinea, Guinea Bissau, Malawi, Sao Tome, and Sierra Leone). This will cost, in total, around about $55bn.

That, at first glance, seems relatively laudable. But really it's not that helpful. Adding all of the debt African countries owe to external countries and bodies, we get to $300bn. This is aid worth $55bn, and Bolivia, Guyana, and Honduras aren't actually in Africa. So it probably leaves Africa around $250bn in debt. ActionAid reckon that there's another forty countries that need immediate 100% debt relief.

And as a sidenote, how many of those people walking round wearing white bands supporting this kind of action could point on a map to any of the countries named above? Some people would say that's irrelevant and that they are showing caring for people rather than demonstrating their geographical knowledge. But the campaign is a political one. How can they possibly support a particular political campaign if they don't understand its mechanisms and implications, and can't even place the countries on a map?

Back to the point… Compared to what's gone before, this debt relief is a pretty big leap. But far more needs to be done to make a huge impact, and I hope that the G8 will throw up some bigger and brighter ideas. Whether debt relief is the best way of helping these countries is also open to question, and I have to say that I'm not convinced. We need much more open public education and debate on these issues. The campaign should be raising awareness and educating, not just asking people to send letters that they quite possibly don't understand to Tony Blair.

Essentially, whilst the action that's been taken is clearly laudable, a lot more must be done, and it's not time yet to rest and feel good about ourselves. Hundreds of thousands of people die needlessly every day, and this won't stop that. We just have to hope that one of the great minds of our generation can think of a real solution, and that the conscience of the world will lead us to implement it - even at great cost.

/ Posted 11th June 2005

Does the G8 summit matter?

The G8 is one of the few groups which truly has the power to change the world at the stroke of a pen. But, despite their huge wealth, they won't.

Even if these largely Westernised countries offer enormous aid to those most in need, their inability to see the world from the eyes of the desperate will hinder any attempt to help: They are far to focused on Western cultures and ways of approaching problems to provide genuine solutions. They can't even agree that condoms are the best way of preventing the spreading of HIV, despite mountains of evidence proving this, so how on Earth do they hope to tackle the far trickier problems of poverty?

But just because these countries can't get together and change the world for the better doesn't mean that we should write the G8 off as useless. However unproductive, argumentative, and ineffective the meetings are, we should celebrate the fact that at least these eight leading nations are co-operating and even holding meetings in an age of cynicism, distrust, and warfare.

Achievements aren't everything. The symbolism is just as important. That's why, now more than ever, the G8 summit really matters.

/ Posted 29th June 2005

So did the G8 matter?

A little over a week ago, I argued that the symbolism of the G8 was far more important that anything it would achieve. Now that the summit is over, the final communiqué has been issued, and the leaders are on their way home, have my opinions changed?

In my last piece, I pretty much wrote off anything the G8 would achieve in terms of African poverty, since I thought that

> They are far to focused on Western cultures and ways of approaching problems to provide genuine solutions.

Whilst I still believe that, I think that real steps forward in the aid that is given to these countries have been made. There have been big pledges for increased monetary aid, not least in terms of $1.5bn per year to help to combat malaria - an easily preventable and treatable disease that kills a shameful number of people each year in sub-Saharan African. But aid will still remain below the UN target levels - instead of wanting to exceed the expectations placed upon us by the world in terms of helping other nations, we're not even shamed enough by the current lack to come up to scratch and give what's expected of us. Every step in the right direction helps, but every step not taken results in the deaths of thousands, and I just hope that in future that our government will support African governments in the ways that *they themselves* decide they need help to make their own countries better places.

On climate change, the communiqué is generally full of lots of non-committal bumph, generally about waiting for technology to provide the solution to all our problems instead of taking pro-active measures to reduce carbon emissions with the technology we currently have available. This is, of course, a valid strategy, and if the technology does indeed rescue us then it will provide the most effective solution. But it seems foolish to stake the future of the planet on such a gamble, and I think that it would be more wise to look at cutting greenhouse gases here and now, if only as a backup which may appear to represent a foolish overspend in future if the technology does come along to solve the problem.

In my opinion, not much has really changed policy wise at the G8 summit, especially when you consider that this was a summit of countries with the financial power that these have. But last time I suggested that

> Achievements aren't everything. The symbolism is just as important... we should celebrate the fact that at least these eight leading nations are co-operating and even holding meetings in an age of cynicism, distrust, and warfare.

Of course, I wrote that before yesterday's terrible attacks on London, and it would be lovely if I could now say that the symbolism of these countries standing firm together against the attackers only heightened the point. But, for me, it didn't. I have to say that I personally was disturbed to see eight of the most powerful men on Earth standing united against 'terrorism'. Terrorism is subjective: One man's terrorist is another man's freedom fighter. To see, therefore, eight men resolutely determined to fight an abstract subjective concept filled me with fear far more that it did confidence and peace.

Clearly, if the G8 nations were on the verge of all-out war, the world would be worse-off, and of course we should celebrate co-operation between these nations - and, indeed, between all nations. But we should not support this open declaration of 'War on Terror'. Warring against a concept is not just illogical, it's also dangerous, particular with such a subjective concept. One would have hoped that the meeting of the eight greatest minds of a generation would have reached that conclusion, and the fact that it actually reached the opposite conclusion is cause for concern indeed. Of course all of the nations should condemn the callous attacks on London, resulting in the deaths of scores of people, but it is difficult to do so convincingly on the ground of 'fighting terror' when many of the countries around the table are active engaging in a form of terror in Iraq, killing many times more Iraqi civilians. Why should the lives of citizens of the G8 nations be worth more than the lives of other human beings? Are we not all the same?

Following the G8 summit, I've been left feeling more uncertain about the value of the G8, and a little more concerned about its power and potential for destruction. We can only hope that the leaders choose to use their undeniable powers wisely… not something with which they have a good track record.

/ Posted 8th July 2005

The Downfall of Tony Blair

Tony Blair has become the face of personality politics, and has precipitated one of the most fascinating changes in public perception that I can recall. He was hailed as the everyman hero of the people when he came to power in 1997, yet he will leave office in 2007 as a figure of hate. Charting his downfall over his final years in office has been very revealing.

Mr Blair, how much you have changed

Mr Blair claims to be 'desperately sorry' for the police killing - murder, if you will - of a completely innocent man. I don't question that - I'm sure it was very difficult news for him to hear. However, this isn't the only claim Mr Blair made:

> I understand entirely the feelings of the young man's family.

How can Mr Blair, with his family comfortably tucked away in the Downing Street green zone, possibly even begin to appreciate, let alone understand, the pain of a parent whose child has been brutally murdered under the accepted government policy of a foreign nation? I certainly can't even being to imagine how I'd feel, and I certainly can't claim to understand it. How can Mr Blair?

Who does 'Tony' think he's kidding when he says that he feels Londoners need to stay strong, be brave, and continue with their every day lives, whilst he's stood surrounded by more layers of security than any other individual in the country? It's very easy for him to get back to normal when his transport arrangements include bullet-proof government cars, rather than crowded tube trains. He tries to evoke 'Blitz spirit', whilst simultaneously removing himself from any personal risk. He tries to convince us that 'we're all in this together', and doesn't realise how disingenuous it makes him sound.

How far Mr Blair has come from that moment in 1997 when the fresh-faced Prime Minister spoke in real unity with the citizens he leads when giving his reaction to the death of Diana. He has now seemingly forgotten what it is to be a 'normal' person. No longer Mr Blair the 'pretty straight sort of guy', now Mr Blair the devious statesman. My, how he's changed.

/ Posted 25th July 2005

Soulless

Watching the Prime Minister on *Sunday AM* this morning was depressing. To think he was just eight years ago the fresh-faced everyman who would change the face of politics – 'a pretty straight sort of guy' - is nothing short of tragic.

This morning, he stumbled over even the most simple questions about his innermost beliefs - clearly not struggling to express himself because of enthusiasm, but struggling to remember the prepared answer the focus groups told him he needed to spout. When faced with the tough questioning over Iraq, he largely ignored the questions posed in order to give his own egotistical speech. He looked disinterested, bored, and above all, exhausted. This is not the 'Great Leader' elected in 1997 - this man could hardly be further than that. He's not even effectively manipulating the media any more - when questioned about stepping down, he replied (I'm paraphrasing) that *he* knew what he was going to do, but he wasn't going to tell *us* lowly mortals. Eight years ago, he wouldn't have dreamed of making that so obvious - he'd have given a crowd-pleasing non-answer, not taunted the interviewer.

The questions about the BBC's coverage of Hurricane Katrina were met with the worst of all answers - He could have easily stuck to the 'private conversation' line, he could have given a flattering answer about the Beeb not covering things as he saw it, but the Beeb being impartial and him perhaps being more personally involved, or he could have simply chosen not to answer at all, saying that it was not his place to comment on the Beeb's editorial decisions. Instead, he chose the worst bits of all of those options, saying that it was a private conversation but then divulging details of it anyway, and openly criticising the BBC all at the same time. That's not the Blairite way.

Of course, there could be greater forces at work here, with the PM intentionally being painted as weak and over the hill in political terms, so that Gordon Brown's confident conference speech will make him look like the natural successor. That's one suggestion I can't even entertain. Mr Blair couldn't play down the statesman in himself intentionally even if he wanted to. He thinks he's bigger than his party, and certainly his place in history is more important to him than the future electability of his party.

So what's going on? Blair's lost his touch, he's drained, and ultimately, his eight years at the top have left him completely soulless, more a creation of spin-doctors than a real human being. He climbed the ladder for what he saw as the good of the country, attempting to be the great saviour. But he lost himself along the way, and allowed the advisers with which he surrounded himself destroy his very person. How very Shakespearean; how very tragic.

/ Posted 25th September 2005

'Just a one-off'

One of the biggest belly-laughs of the day comes courtesy of the Prime Minister's Official Spokesman quoted by the Press Association:

> "He will make sure he does vote in future on important votes," said Mr Blair's official spokesman. "This was a one-off."

His failure to vote on his 'crucial' Racial Hatred Bill was apparently a one-off occasion on which Mr Blair has missed an important vote. Presumably, the September 1998 vote to cut student funding, the April 2000 vote on the Freedom of Information legislation, the January 2001 vote to ban hunting with dogs, the November 2001 vote on Afghanistan airstrikes, the November 2001 vote on anti-terror legislation, the February 2002 vote on single-faith schools, the March 2002 vote on the licensing of hunting with dogs, the February 2003 House of Lords reform vote, the June 2003 vote on hunting with dogs, and the December 2004 ID cards vote - all of which were variously described as 'important' or 'crucial' votes - were just one-off occasions where the PM didn't bother voting too.

In fact, he has the worst voting record of any modern PM, turning up for just 94 out of 1250 votes in the last Parliament - a pitiful 7.5% attendance rate. Most MPs, by comparison, turn up for about 65% of votes.

So really, the fact he bothered to turn up for the first vote was more of a one-off.

/ Posted 1st February 2006

The end for Blair?

So Blair has come third in the local elections. That's not good for him. In response to this, and the scandals surround the Labour party for last fortnight, he's performed a reshuffle so huge that it begins to feel like he's got a whole new deck. Charles Clarke has been unceremoniously sacked, saying that he disagrees with Blair, and Prescott is angry too at the prospect of losing the bigger part of his responsibility whilst retaining his title and his salary. If that happened to me, I certainly wouldn't be angry, I'd probably be cheering, but that's Prescott for you.

Patricia Hewitt has retained her post, despite the service that she is trying to reform revolting against her, and losing all faith in her abilities. And Jack Straw, who's seemingly done nothing wrong, gets demoted. Sensible.

Earlier in the week, I couldn't understand why Clarke hadn't resigned. It would now appear that he genuinely believed he could carry on. This was actually good news for Mr Blair, because it meant he had a big headline-grabber for election results day, so the fact that Labour have performed appallingly could be buried.

Yesterday, I was unsure whether he'd pulled off something incredible, and made a fantastic political play, or whether this really would be the beginning of the end. But the news today that in a week's time, seventy-five backbench MPs are to deliver a letter telling him to resign or he will be challenged changes everything. This simply isn't how Blair wanted to go.

Blair and Brown are holding talks this weekend about the future of the party. Basically, it's pretty clear that they're talking about when Blair should go. On Monday, Blair has a press conference at which this topic surely can't be ignored. But what can Blair do now? If he resigned next week, he'd look pressured into it, which isn't what he wants to do - he wants to go according to his own timetable. If he leaves it much longer, he will be forced out by his own party. If he announces a future resignation date, perhaps there's scope for a few headlines now about him being forced out, but at the time of the transition of power, perhaps that will be more forgotten.

Could he announce that he'll stand down on his tenth anniversary as Prime Minister? That would give about a year for the transition to take place, satisfy most of the party, and make it look like he was going according to his own timetable. It would also allow him the honour of making an official 'final' conference speech without plotters murmuring in the background. If backbenchers are more insistent, he could always announce that he'll leave at the end of the year, which would have similar advantages.

But, of course, announcing in advance makes him a true lame duck, something that he and the party would probably object to over such a long period. So what can he do? Probably very little. He's been greedy, and left the transition too long for it to happen in any symbolic, pretty way.

The idea that he won't get his last wish after nearly a decade of leadership almost makes me feel sorry for him. Almost.

/ Posted 6th May 2006

Blair will 'depart' within a year

I've never considered Blair to be one of the greatest orators to have occupied Number 10, but maybe I've underestimated him. It's quite impressive to see him give a full statement about leaving office without using the word 'resign'. Or even 'quit' or 'leave'. The nearest thing he's given to a soundbite is

> The next party conference in a couple of weeks will be my last party conference as party leader.

He's even managed to rush the sentence so much that it can't realistically be used as a soundbite. That's pretty impressive, and very well done. Is this this the first speech Tony's done where he's consciously avoided the soundbite?

Quite honestly, though, I don't think it matters. I think even the smallest of the Labour minnows will not be put off from making their views on his Premiership clear just because he says it's wrong to do so now, and even the super-loyal MPs trotted out across every network immediately after the speech to scare them a little more won't make them feel threatened.

Mr Blair's statement has put a sticking plaster over his gaping wounds, the question is merely how long it will last. It won't last seven or eight months. It only needs one comment from one MP, one letter, or one more resignations to painfully tear the sticking plaster away, and it's just too tempting.

It was a valiant effort, though, and I'm rather impressed. Just not impressed enough to want him to stay.

/ Posted 7th September 2006

For the good of us all, Blair must fall

In the UK, the government is in crisis. And yet Blair insists on hanging on, and has indicated he still hopes to be Prime Minister at the end of June. Why, oh why, won't he just do the honourable thing and *go now*?

The Home Office is in a terrible state. It's lost control of immigration, asylum, prisons, and is interfering in judicial sentencing. A catalogue of blunders recently have shown us that they haven't tracked criminals who have committed crimes abroad, they've lost contact with 322 convicted sex offenders who they're supposed to be monitoring in this country, they're illegally locking up asylum seekers who've done nothing wrong, they haven't enforced travel bans where they should have, prisons are bursting at the seams, the head of the Youth Justice board has resigned in disgust, they've lost terror suspects, and now John Reid is sending letters to judges - interfering in their ability to judge properly - telling them to send only the 'most serious' offenders to prison - then saying that this means exactly the same as saying that people who post 'any risk' to the public should be locked up. Apparently 'most serious' and 'serious' and synonymous in the lexis of our Home Secretary. Oh, and this disaster of a department still wants us all to trust it with ID cards, which will run on *current systems*. Which have been oh-so-successful.

On top of that, the NHS is in a terrible state, with more doctors going to be out of work any time soon thanks to MMC meaning there aren't enough jobs to go round, and a Health Secretary who believes we have too many doctors and that last year was the 'best ever' for the NHS. Patricia Hewitt announced she'd get NHS debt under control, and it doubled to half a billion pounds - yet this was seen as good progress, despite being twice as much debt as her target amount. The staff of the NHS have lost confidence in her and want her to resign, but Mr Blair continues to back her to the hilt. Oh, and she wants to criminalise any staff who are still there, and she thinks GPs are overpaid - despite it being her who decided how much they were paid.

Let's not forget that inflation is at 3% - the highest rate for 11 years, we're still fighting a war in Iraq which was all about weapons of mass destruction that didn't exist, and the Ministry of Defence can't even look after soldiers properly. The Prime Minister himself is at the centre of a criminal investigation, with his closest advisers arrested and the net closing in on the PM himself.

Despite all this, Mr Blair thinks he can continue. He's 'not finished yet'. He genuinely believes he's the right person to lead a party into elections.

Surely Mr Blair can see that his administration is a disaster. Surely he can see that a new administration is needed to even have a hope of clearing up the mess created by this one. So please, Mr Blair, go soon, and let us get on with repairing the damage caused under your arrogant and destructive leadership.

/ Posted 28th January 2007

Mr Blair: A man of a different era

On a morning when polls show that Labour are at a record low with the electorate, Mr Blair took the opportunity to attack the Tories, calling them 'confused'.

> Every time they are called on to make a big judgement call on policy, they misfire. New Labour made the Tories lose their bearings and this new Tory leadership has not found them. From law and order, to NHS reform, to taxes on the environment, they just get it wrong.

Politics is cyclical. New Labour, with the help of Mr Blair, introduced a breath of simplicity to the system. He brought us back to black-and-white, good-and-bad, right-and-wrong politics, which fitted with a popularity for that kind of thinking in the country at large.

Mr Cameron has reintroduced the era of nuanced politics. The era of greys, where some parts of something can be right, while other parts are wrong. An era where decisions are difficult and finely balanced between benefit and risk. And, once again, we're starting to see a popularity for that kind of thing in the country at large.

Mr Blair rubbishing all of Mr Cameron's ideas as without merit belongs to an earlier political era, and makes him look silly - especially when Mr Cameron is capable of working with the government on parts of plans he believes are right.

It's startling to see a Grand Master of the political game suddenly unable to keep up with a new young upstart.

/ Posted 20th April 2007

Adios, Anthony – It wasn't all bad

Everybody with the ability to communicate appears to be commenting today on Tony Blair's legacy today, after he announced that he would resign on 27th July.

It's easy to point out that he's buried bad news to the end, choosing to use the day of an interest rate rise to announcing his 'departure timetable', something perhaps more familiar to a steam train than a politician. Not to mention the burying of the news that the cost of the ID card scheme has increased by £840m.

It's easy to point out that he's the King of Soundbites to the end: 'The best nation on Earth'.

It's easy to point out that his departure had the same theme tune as his arrival, *Things Can Only Get Better*, and wonder when it was most true.

It's all-to-easy for people like me to knock Blair's achievement. We can criticise him for his sofa-style of government, his five wars, his failures.

But for all his faults, he is the first Labour Leader to secure three successive election victories. He has introduced policies which have made the country better - the minimum wage being a case in point. He is the first 'celebrity' Prime Minister. And he's a very successful politician.

His legacy will be the war in Iraq - his biggest failure. His defence of his less successful policies – 'I did what I thought was right' - reveals, perhaps, his biggest failing: Government should not take decisions based upon the whim of the Prime Minister - however well intentioned - but on the facts, considered opinion from experts in their field, Cabinet discussion and debate, and Parliamentary process.

It's a legacy, but not, I think, the one he wanted.

/ Posted 10th May 2007

Robert Kilroy-Silk

If Tony Blair's downfall has been the modern-day equivalent of a Greek tragedy, then Robert Kilroy-Silk's return to politics has been the modern-day equivalent of the performance of a court jester. I can't think of anyone who has made quite such an idiot of themselves through the medium of politics in recent years, and these posts explain why.

Kilroy-Silk quits 'shameful' UKIP

Surely this idiot has finally lost every scintilla of credibility he ever had… not that he had much to start with. To appear to quit a party simply because they won't make him leader, and then to set up his own party, is quite insane. I think he's very wrong to think that people voted for UKIP as a vote for him: People voted for UKIP because they liked what UKIP stood for, and his campaigning brought light to those policies. I can't see voters now following him to a new party led entirely by him, because it will be even less credible than UKIP.

This is very good news for the main political parties, though: There was some danger that UKIP would take votes away from them, but with all this squabbling and silliness going on I can't see anyone voting for UKIP or Veritas.

/ Posted on 20th January 2005

Kilroy-Silk promises surprises with his new party

The surprise being that it'll be composed entirely of trans-sexuals who are having affairs with homosexual dwarves? That's what I'd guess. After all, that's the kind of person he'd be used to, after all his TV work.

How can he possibly believe that this little party of his is ever going to get anywhere? He's a delusional fool. But I'll be watching the party launch (if anybody's showing it) for the comedy value.

/ Posted on 2nd February 2005

No-one quits quicker than a Kilroy quitter

First, he quit his TV show before the BBC pushed him. Then he quit UKIP before the leadership pushed him (leading me to say 'Surely this idiot has finally lost every scintilla of credibility he ever had'). Now, he's quit his own party, set up only six months ago, before the membership pushed him. Oh, and now he's being encouraged to quit as an MEP. It's probably for the best. We couldn't have him breaking with form. And to think, I called him a 'delusional fool' when he said he'd change the face of British politics. Could I have been more wrong?

When he joined UKIP, Kilroy said:

> [People are] fed up with being lied to ... fed up with being patronised by the metropolitan elite

At the launch of his party, Kilroy said:

> People are fed up with the old parties and lies and deception.

Today, he said:

> [T]he electors are content with the old parties and ... it would be virtually impossible for a new party to make a significant impact

It's good to have a fun story in a month that's been so difficult. And Kilroy is certainly nothing more than a figure of fun.

The question now is: Where does Kilroy go next? Will he quit politics altogether? Perhaps he'll become the new face of Orange. / *Posted 29th July 2005*

The Best of the Rest

Not everything on sjhoward.co.uk is political. That'd just be dull. So here's a selection of seven of the best of all the other, non-politics, posts that have appeared on sjhoward.co.uk in the last four years.

Trip to Safeway

Clutching the list provided by my mother, I leapt in the car and navigated my way to Safeway, about 10 minutes or so away. This was difficult enough in itself, what with idiots being unable to indicate correctly and others who decide to slam on their brakes at the last minute, deciding in the last second that yes they do want to turn, and further idiots who decide that the speed limits don't apply to them and so insist on driving in my boot. Why do these numbskulls insist on complaining to the *Daily Mail* when a speed camera catches them breaking the law and they get fined? The equation is simple: You *exceed* the *limit* - yes, it's a *limit* - and you get a *fine.* Don't complain about the speed cameras, if you want fewer of them about then *stop speeding* and they'll soon stop erecting them because they'll have no fines to fund them. Anyway, back to the point.

I eventually arrive just about in one piece at Safeway, and decide to choose a parking space. I select one, and drive into it. I can't drive into it fully, thanks to Safeway's idea of putting trees inside rhomboidal paving areas in the middle of four adjoining spaces (I'm sure they do this just to laugh when you forget it's there and hence think you can drive through the space in front to get out - and inevitably, you hit the kerb). Some fool then decides to pull into the space next to me - nay, he pulls half into *my* space, almost preventing me from being able to get *out* of my car. Nevertheless, I soldier on.

I enter the store and select a trolley. I would complain that it had a wonky wheel, but it didn't. It was however very wet, having been out in the rain. Why the trolley collectors are incapable of putting the dry trolleys in one column, and then placing the wet ones in another column, I'll never know. I always used to when I worked at Homebase. Instead, they trap the only dry trolleys behind a fleet of dripping trolleys, forcing you to push a freezing, soaking metal basket around the shop.

And the first section one finds in the shop? Fruit. Why, oh why do supermarkets always have fruit near the door? It inevitably ends up at the bottom of the trolley bashed in. And it doesn't make me want to buy more, or anything like that. It's just another daily annoyance.

Then you try and navigate the aisles. This is made difficult by the very idea of shopping. People park their trolleys (why isn't it 'trollies'?) at the edges of the aisles. Once you've got two trolleys parked opposite each other, the aisles are simply not wide enough to get another through the middle. This fills me with trolley rage.

The first item on the list is 'Benecol Yoghurt'. So I proceed with earnest to the dairy aisle. Yoghurt being a dairy product, this doesn't seem an unreasonable assumption. And I was right. I was presented with a myriad of yoghurts. These were not shelved logically, for example 'Plain Yoghurts' and 'Fruit Yoghurts', instead I'm forced to decide whether Benecol is an 'Everyday Yoghurt', an 'Adult Yoghurt', a 'Children's Yoghurt', or a 'Dessert Yoghurt'. I walk down this aisle five times, scanning all of the products looking for the mystical Benecol. I then admit defeat and ask for assistance. I am directed to 'Yoghurt Drinks'. When I question this logic, I'm told 'It's there because Benecol also do a yoghurt drink, and the yoghurts are next to that'. I sigh, and proceed as directed, to discover that they've sold out of the yoghurt in question.

Item two: 'One loaf of Hovis Best of Both'. I walk to the bread section, singing this to myself (I really have started talking to myself an awful lot recently, is this a sign of insanity?). I discover that there is a whole aisle dedicated to loaves of bread. Why? What can possibly be the difference between all these different types of sliced bread? Can anybody actually tell the difference between Safeway Long Life Sliced White and Warburtons White Sliced Toaster Bread? I mean, for goodness sake, what is the difference between bread and toaster bread? It surely can't be long before I find that spreads come with a list of 'compatible breads', or something similar. I eventually locate the Best of Both, a ridiculously overpriced product that probably has no health benefits compared to Value Sliced White, under a large sign shouting 'NO BITS!'

Even buying milk is becoming more complex, with the choices of skimmed, semi-skimmed, or full cream now extended to organic and breakfast milk too. What on Earth is breakfast milk? Do they feed the cows Special K or something?

I also discovered that Ainsley Harriot has brought out his own line of teabags. Why? I have no idea. I'm I the only person in the country that doesn't associate Ainsley Harriot with teabags?

I eventually make my way to the checkout, being careful not to select one marked 'Baskets Only' or '9 items or fewer' (at least they get their signs right), and load my shopping onto the conveyer belt. The assistant then decides she'll have a lengthy conversation with another member of staff about the fact she's only got five minutes left and she's going out to get hammered tonight.

Eventually, she decides to serve me, if I can call it that, by scanning my products and throwing them at me as I try and pack them into plastic bags. She tries to strike up conversation, saying 'Oh, do you like Best of Both? Doesn't it taste funny?'

It's all I can do not to respond sarcastically, saying that I hate it. I just smile and say yes. The transaction is completed, and I'm handed a receipt which must have taken half the Brazilian rainforests to produce, what with its Petrol Payback voucher and other extraneous bits and bobs.

I then push my trolley to the car, and load my stuff into the boot. I then walk half way home trying to find a trolley park to dump my trolley, before hopping in the car and trying to go home. Why trying? Because I sensibly follow the arrows to the Exit only to find that they don't actually lead to the exit. I challenge anyone who lives in Southport to visit Safeway, and follow the exit arrows. You eventually come to one that point that opposite way to that you are driving. They do not make sense. So after a tour of the car park, I give up and just drive in the general direction of the exit.

I leave, kindly allowing someone out in front of me, and make my way home with a newfound hate, deeper than ever, for supermarket shopping.

/ Posted 14th January 2004

Celebrities unite to help New Orleans' pets

It's the kind of story you really couldn't make up. Parody has merged with reality, as Stella McCartney and Pamela Anderson unite to help the domestic pets affected by Hurricane Katrina.

Thousands of people are dead, and hundreds of thousands are homeless in what's been described as the USA's greatest ever disaster. Billions of pounds of damage has been caused, the area is in chaos with looting and shootings seemingly common.

People have lost their entire life's possessions, and all the memories associated with them. Even Michael Jackson's getting stuck in to the humanitarian aid effort. And two slightly ditsy blondes want to help the cats, dogs, and guinea pigs of the region.

I'm sure they'll be grateful.

/ Posted 7th September 2005

West Virginia mining disaster

This story of members of miners' families being told that they were alive, only for it to turn out that the information was wrong, and all but one had died, is clearly tragic, and my thoughts are with the family and friends of the dead.

But one small thing struck me: When it was falsely announced that the miners were alive, the assembled crowds thanked God. When it was announced that a mistake had been made and the men were actually dead, they blamed the company. I just thought that was an interesting disparity - make of it what you will.

/ Posted 4th January 2006

US attack on TV gay icon

Last time I chceked, tolerance was a key plank of the Christian religion. So why is it a problem if SpongeBob Squarepants is spreading a message of tolerance of homosexuals? Kids are not going to magically 'turn' gay because a heroic sponge is a bit camp.

And how did a cartoon sponge that wears clothes and lives in a pineapple under the sea ever make such a big splash (pun intended) over the pond (I can't help it) as to make our broadsheets? Do conservative American Christians really not have anything else they could be rallying against? Are there no bigger fish to fry? Like 'One nation, under God' launching illegal and unjust wars? Or that their country is leading the world towards the destruction of God's planet?

One of the biggest problems with America today is that they have confused Christianity and patriotism: Quite an achievement for a country that fiercely defends the separation of Church and State. If you're not Christian, then you're anti-American, which is how much of America can justify attacks on Iraq.

Surely the leader of a truly Christian nation would end all speeches with 'Praise be to God in the highest', or some other offering of praise, not a request that 'God Bless America', which inevitably and inextricably links politics and religion, and offers no pacification to a God that supposedly has the power to cause eternal pain.

Frankly, if I believed in that God, I wouldn't be able to conduct my daily life without fear, as everything I did would have to be out of obsessive compulsion to please, or not offend, God. In my opinion, it would be impossible to conduct a normal life with such a belief, let alone to lead a nation. So perhaps Bush doesn't believe quite as much as he'd like us to think.

/ *Posted 22nd January 2005*

World's most famous couple together again

You'll remember Valentine's 2004. It was the year that the world's most famous celebrity couple split, a spokesperson saying that they were to 'spend some quality time apart'. But it was widely known that Barbie had dumped Ken - her lover of forty-three years - for Blaine, an Australian 'boogie surf boarder' she met on a trip to California.

But now, two years on, he's back. Ken has got back up, dusted himself down (with a little help from the Hollywood stylist Phillip Bloch), and the couple are said to be romantically involved once again. A lot has changed for Ken in the last couple of years - he's been off on a self-reflection trip around Europe and the far-east, and seems to have matured somewhat, preferring Norah Jones to his pop-filled past, and becoming a bit rougher around the edges, with ripped jeans and unkempt hair. It's all in sharp contrast to Blaine's perfected, obsessive self-styling.

So the romance is back on, after a two-year separation. But what's become of Blaine? Nobody seems to have any comment to make. It seems this home-wrecker has gone into hiding for now, at least. Perhaps he just couldn't compete - after all, most of us would love to look like Barbie and Ken when we're in our fifties - perhaps he was already starting to age.

Hmm… What *am* I doing with my life?

/ Posted 10th February 2006

The 'Goth' subculture

In Tuesday's *G2*, Dave Simpson argued that the Goth subculture amongst sections of today's youth is probably a good thing. Quoting an academic from Sussex University:

> Most youth subcultures encourage people to drop out of school and do illegal things. Most goths are well educated, however. They hardly ever drop out and are often the best pupils. The subculture encourages interest in classical education, especially the arts. I'd say goths are more likely to make careers in web design, computer programming ... even journalism.

This is not normally the kind of thing I'd pick up on. I knew many goths, but could never claim to have been one. However, something does quite regularly strike me. Often, on a Wednesday, I trundle back from my morning in GP Land and stop off at Sainsbury's to pick up some groceries and other sundries. Now, my local branch of Sainsbury's (which is laid out most oddly, but that's by-the-by) is just down the road from the local Sixth Form College, and many of the students pop down there to purchase their lunch (and they might possible pick up some other sundries too).

As I've shopped, I've become increasingly aware of the disdainful attitude of the staff and other customers towards these youths - some of whom are dressed in the Gothic style. This is despite that fact that during my regular visits, I have never - *never* - seen any of the pupils misbehaving in the shop. Yes, they're boisterous and occasionally loud, but that's not really doing anyone any harm. I can quite easily pick up my shopping with no trouble whatsoever. And yet these young people are tutted at, often stalked by staff, and generally treated as second-class citizens. This is based purely on their profile as young people.

I ask you, if the staff of Sainsbury's had a similarly negative attitude towards elderly people, would it be acceptable? Certainly not. And yet the elderly cause more logistical headaches for the supermarket than do the young people, through no fault of their own. They tend to require more assistance, and tend to spend longer in the shop, for example. The basis for the blatant discrimination against the young people appears to be a popular stereotype perpetuated by the popular press, and no-one complains about this. Society views youngsters and a nuisance, not recognising that these are the doctors, lawyers, and priests of the future, whilst simultaneously rejecting the disrespect of the elderly based on their past lives as doctors, lawyers, and priests. And yet surely it is more logical to respect someone for what they have the potential to become than to respect them for what they have been, and will never be again.

If a section of the community is not respected, then respect is not fostered within that group. If we insist on discriminating against and criminalising the harmless, natural activities of the teenagers of this country, then we cause more problems than we solve. So next time you see a 'goth', or read about some kid being given an 'ASBO', please look beyond the stereotype, and respect that the individual you're tutting at today might well be caring for you tomorrow.

/ Posted 22nd March 2006

Humphrey has died

Humphrey, Chief Mouser to the Cabinet Office, has died aged 78*. Possibly the most interesting of the former inhabitants of Downing Street, he was drafted in a year after the retirement of the previous incumbent of his post, Wilberforce, in 1987 following 70 years' faithful service.

Humphrey combined the Blairite spirit of social mobility (homeless to Minister) and Thatcherite cost-cutting (£3900 off the Downing Street pest-control bill) long before David Cameron even thought about cutting his political teeth.

Like most Downing Street residents, Humphrey was involved in many scandals during his political life. In 1994, he was falsely accused of murder, leading Prime Minister John Major to personally protest his innocence. The very next year, he was found to be 'missing, presumed dead', though three months later was found to have been merely holidaying at the Royal Army Medical College. This discovery lead to him releasing his first, and only, public statement to the press:

> I have had a wonderful holiday at the Royal Army Medical College, but it is nice to be back and I am looking forward to the new parliamentary session.

Things were relatively stable in Humphrey's life until the upheaval caused by Labour's election in 1997, which badly shook Humphrey, and led his long-term kidney condition to worsen. He was forced to retire later that same year, though controversy still surrounds the issue of his departure: Some say that Cherie Blair insisted on his retirement, though this has been consistently denied.

Even in retirement, scandal was never far away: Shortly after Humphrey's retirement, Alan Clark MP alleged that he had been assassinated by the incoming Labour government, and demanded evidence that this wasn't the case. Of course, Humphrey was more than happy to oblige, but valuing his privacy insisted on a photo-shoot at a secret location, picturing him with a stack of the day's newspapers. Many cruelly commented that he appeared to be putting on weight in retirement, and these comments led to Humphrey retiring completely and permanently from the media spotlight.

In 2005, Humphrey was briefly back in the news, with an attempt to discover his whereabouts using the Freedom of Information Act. These efforts were largely fruitless, though *The Independent* did claim to discover that he was alive and well.

Earlier this week, the Downing Street Press Office announced the sad death of Humphrey saying that he 'sadly died last week some time'. To think that one of (if not the) longest serving resident of Downing Street was not honoured in any way, or even given the dignity of a proper announcement of the date of his death, is rather distressing. One would hope that, after so many false announcements and presumptions of death throughout his life, when it finally did come, he would be properly respected. But it was not to be.

Requiescat in pace

/ Posted 21st March 2006

*That's cat years, of course

www.ingramcontent.com/pod-product-compliance
Ingram Content Group UK Ltd.
Pitfield, Milton Keynes, MK11 3LW, UK
UKHW041948190726
13854UKWH00004B/1856

9 781847 534460